HOW TO TEACH ABOUT VALUES:

An Analytic Approach

JACK R. FRAENKEL

San Francisco State University

Prentice-Hall, Inc.
Englewood Cliffs, New Jersey 07632

Library of Congress Cataloging in Publication Data

Fraenkel, Jack R
  How to teach about values.

  Bibliography: p. 149
  1. Moral education. I. Title.
LC268.F72   370.11'4   76-30448
ISBN 0-13-435446-X
    0-13-435453-2 (pbk.)

PRINTED IN THE UNITED STATES OF AMERICA

10 9 8 7 6 5 4 3 2 1

Prentice-Hall International, Inc., *London*
Prentice-Hall of Australia Pty. Limited, *Sydney*
Prentice-Hall of Canada, Ltd., *Toronto*
Prentice-Hall of India Private Limited, *New Delhi*
Prentice-Hall of Japan, Inc., *Tokyo*
Prentice-Hall of Southeast Asia Pte. Ltd., *Singapore*
Whitehall Books Limited, *Wellington, New Zealand*

CONTENTS

iii

PREFACE

This book has been written for teachers, teachers-to-be, curriculum workers, professors of education, or anyone else who might be interested in teaching about values. My intent has been to present a simple and straightforward explanation of some procedures and techniques which I believe values education should include. These procedures and techniques are based on the belief that being able to identify, analyze, and assess alternative policies and procedures, along with their consequences, intelligently (that is, rationally), is an important ability for all people to possess. For to the extent that a person is *not* aware of certain options that might be pursued in a particular situation, to that extent is he or she restricted in the choices that might be made, where choice is possible. The ideas and strategies presented in this book, therefore, are based on the assumption that a continuing analysis and assessment of alternatives in schools can help to develop this ability.

This is *not* to say that the identification and analysis of alternatives and consequences is all there is to values education. Other techniques and procedures, including some suggested by those who wish primarily to "clarify" values or develop "moral reasoning" are worthy of consideration. But few, if any, of the procedures and techniques developed by advocates of these approaches attempt to deal in any sort of sustained or explicit way with the exploration and assessment of consequences. Such exploration and assessment, however, is vital to intelligent choosing from among alternatives, since the past, present, or possible effects of an action determine, to a considerable extent, its desirability.

The main purpose of this book, like everything that I write, is to make you think a bit. If it succeeds in this regard, the book will have served its purpose, and I shall be pleased.

JACK R. FRAENKEL
San Francisco, California

chapter one

VALUES AND SCHOOLING

- In Chicago, Illinois, a biology teacher vivisects a frog in front of her tenth-grade class.
- In San Francisco, California, a mathematics teacher lectures to his class on the inherent beauty to be found in geometric forms.
- In Atlanta, Georgia, a fourth-grade teacher requires that students raise their hands before they speak out in class discussions.
- In Fremont, Nebraska, a social studies teacher insists that his students "stick to the facts" in their discussion of the causes and effects of the Spanish-American war.
- In Albuquerque, New Mexico, a junior high school teacher devotes one day a week to discussing such topics as alienation, poverty, crime, and drug abuse in her eighth-grade class in American literature.
- In Boston, Massachusetts, a kindergarten teacher holds daily sharing sessions in which the students sit in a circle and try to say "something nice" about the person sitting to their immediate left and right.

Each of the above incidents shows a teacher at work. Each gives us a brief glimpse of a person who, in one way or another, is "teaching." And each tells us a little bit about that person as a human being. Each of these individuals, no doubt, has in mind some objective or goal that he or she is trying to accomplish. A person's goals tell us something about what that person values—what he or she considers important in life. Thus each of these vignettes gives us some idea (though admittedly a very sketchy one) of what each teacher values.

VALUES AND THE SCHOOLS

Teaching is a value-oriented enterprise. The teaching of values, in fact, is unavoidable. All the activities in which teachers engage—the books they ask students to read, the seating arrangements they establish, the

1

topics they choose to discuss, the manner in which they discuss them, the films and filmstrips they select, the speakers they invite, the movies and plays they recommend, the assignments they give, and the examinations they prepare—all these suggest that they consider some ideas, events, individuals, and behaviors more important than others for students to consider.

It is not just teaching that is value impregnated, however. So, too, are the schools as a whole. As John Childs once remarked, the organization of a system of schools is in itself a moral enterprise, for it represents the deliberate attempt of a human society to control the pattern of its own evolution.[1] Values obviously permeate the "formal" curriculum of the school—the deliberately planned-for experiences that are designed to accomplish the intended, though not always explicitly stated, goals of the various areas of the curriculum. However, values *also* are part of the "hidden" curriculum—the experiences that are not planned and that often result in unintended and sometimes undesired student learnings. Consider the following.

- In Des Moines, Iowa, several students wear black armbands for a day as a symbol of protest against the Vietnam War. When asked to remove the armbands, the students refuse and are suspended.[2]
- In San Jose, California, a student applies for admission to one of the city's senior high schools. The registrar informs the student that he cannot be registered until his hair length conforms to the school regulation that states:

A boy's hair shall not fall below the eyes in front and shall not cover the ears, and it shall not extend below the collar in back.

- In Washington, D.C., a school counselor admonishes a boy and a girl not to walk through the halls with their arms around one another because "it doesn't look right."
- In Seattle, Washington, a fourth-grade teacher demands that two students participate more in discussions and "speak up" in class. The parents of the students, who are Buddhists, protest that their sons are rewarded at home for being contemplative.
- In Topeka, Kansas, a physical education teacher prohibits a student from participating in gym activities because the student refuses to take a shower at school. His parents ask that he be excused from showering,

---

[1] John L. Childs, *Education and Morals* (New York: Appleton-Century Crofts, 1950), pp. 17–19.

[2] This decision, which took place in 1969, was taken to court by the students' parents. The resulting case, *Tinker* v. *Des Moines*, eventually was appealed to the Supreme Court. In a 7–2 decision, the Court ruled that students are "persons" under the Constitution and that under the First Amendment various forms of peaceful protest such as the wearing of armbands qualify for protection as a form of "free speech."

stating that he does so at home. The physical education instructor states that the school has a policy of "no exceptions" in this regard.

- In Seattle, Washington, a teacher rearranges the desks in his classroom into a circle so that more students will be able to participate easily in class discussions. He arrives at school the next morning to find the desks placed again in straight, parallel rows. Upon complaining to the principal, he is told that the desks must be left in rows, because it is too difficult for the custodian to clean around them if they are not so arranged.
- In New Brunswick, New Jersey, teachers are required to punch a time clock before beginning the day's work and at the end of each workday. They are required to be "on duty" at 8:15 A.M. and to remain until 4 P.M. Classes begin at 8:45 A.M. and end at 2:45 P.M.
- In Canon City, Colorado, a teacher is fired for letting her students write graffiti—some of them obscene—on a blackboard. The graffiti had producted an outpouring of negative student sentiment toward the school principal.

What do such actions convey to students about the values of school policy makers in each instance? What do they suggest about the kinds of things those policy makers expect the students themselves to value? There are some basic questions here for all who work in schools to think about. Do the formal and hidden curricula conflict in any ways? The implications of what goes on, both formally and informally, cannot help but give students some ideas about what the school board, the teachers, and the administrators consider important. Is that which is stated and/or implied what teachers and administrators want to stress?

Would it be possible to avoid teaching values in schools? If you think it would be, how could it be avoided?

The point being made here is that "values education" goes on all the time in schools. It permeates not only the curriculum, but also the day-to-day interactions of students and staff.

Fred & Others

© 1973. By permission of Ron Tandberg.

It appears, for example, in the affairs of the playground—in the kind of sports that are favored and opposed, and in the code of sportsmanship by which the young are taught to govern their behavior in the actual play of various games. It appears in the social life of the school—in all of the behaviors that are approved or disapproved as the young are taught the manners—the conventional or minor morals—of their society. It appears in the school's definition of the delinquent and in its mode of dealing with him. It appears in the way children are taught to treat those of different racial, religious, occupational, economic or national backgrounds. It appears in the department of science: in the methods the young are expected to adopt in conducting their experiments, in their reports of what actually happened during the course of their experiments, as well as in the regard of the teachers of science for accuracy, for precision, and for conclusions that are based on objective data rather than on wishful thinking. It appears in the department of social studies: in the problems that are chosen to be discussed, in the manner in which they are discussed, in the historical documents and events that are emphasized, as well as in the leaders that are chosen to illustrate the important and the worthy and the unimportant and the unworthy in the affairs of man. It appears in the department of literature: in the novels, the poems, the dramas that are chosen for study, in what is considered good and what is considered bad in the various forms and styles of human conduct and expression. It appears in the organization and the government of the school: in the part that superintendent, supervisors, teachers, pupils, are expected to play in the making and the maintenance of the regulations of the school. It appears in the methods of grading, promoting, and distributing honors among the children of the school. It appears in the celebration of national holidays: in the particular events that are celebrated as well as in the historical and contemporary personalities who are chosen to exemplify the qualities of citizenship and worthy community service. It appears in the program for the general assemblies of the schools: in the various leaders from the community who are brought in to speak to the children. It appears in the way teachers are treated: the amount of freedom and initiative they enjoy, in the extent to which teachers are permitted to take part in the life of their community, and the degree to which the young believe that they are studying under leaders who are more than docile, routine drill-masters in assigned subjects. It appears in the way the community organizes to conduct its schools: in the provision it makes in its schoolgrounds, buildings, and equipment, in the kind of people it chooses to serve on the school board, and in the relation of the members of the board to the administrative and teaching staff.[3]

[3] John L. Childs, *Education and Morals* (New York: Appleton-Century-Crofts, 1950), pp. 17–19.

As Professor John Childs has written, "The moral factor appears whenever the school, or the individual teacher or supervisor, is *for* certain things and *against* other things." [4] Nevertheless, it must be admitted that the *explicit* consideration of values and value-laden issues on any sort of systematic basis rarely occurs in most schools and classrooms. As indicated above, the discussion and analysis of values still seems to occur implicitly (i.e., through the selection and use of certain books and other materials) rather than deliberately as a result of careful planning and design by teachers and administrators. Why is this?

Many reasons can be offered to explain the fact that most teachers and schools do not engage in systematic values education. Most teachers in the United States today grew up in a culture that traditionally viewed questions of value as essentially private matters not to be discussed in public. Often, parents and other groups of citizens oppose the discussion in schools of controversy, which value issues—by their very nature—involve. Furthermore, some teachers fear that any explicit attempt to develop values or to discuss value issues in the classroom boils down to indoctrination on their part. Many, encouraged in their undergraduate courses to concentrate on "getting the facts," state that they have more than enough to do trying to "get the subject matter across" without having to worry about values. Others believe that values education is more properly the domain of the family or the church. And a few confess that they are ignorant of how to teach about values even if they wished to do so.

Though these objections and fears are understandable, they need not prevent teachers from dealing with values and value issues in their classrooms. First of all, many issues and topics that once were viewed as private matters are now discussed openly in newspapers and magazines. Secondly, teachers can help students to think about and discuss value-laden issues without insisting that a particular point of view or position be endorsed or accepted.

As far as subject matter goes, any subject is loaded with questions and issues about values. To ignore this fact is to ignore much that is rich and vital about the subject. How can one study President Truman's decision to drop the atom bomb on Hiroshima and Nagasaki, Richard Wright's decision to become a thief in *Black Boy,* the area of ecology, the use of drugs, what makes a certain painting "great" or a particular kind of music exciting, teamwork in sports, or classroom rules without referring to values? It is doubtful that one can ignore values in discussing any subject. As mentioned before, the very fact that a teacher chooses certain topics, individuals, places, periods, or events suggests that he or she views some things as more important to study than others.

4 Ibid., p. 17.

The argument that values education more properly belongs in the home or church is a traditional one, but there is little evidence that any sort of *systematic* discussion of values and value issues occurs in these institutions. One must consider that most Americans do not attend church regularly, that few parents are trained in rational value analysis, and that few facilities exist for training parents in discussion skills. It then seems unrealistic to assume that we should rely on the home and church rather than on the school for any sort of comprehensive program of values education.

Finally, even though many teachers have not been trained to discuss values systematically, several strategies and techniques for discussing and analyzing values are available. Like any set of skills, these strategies and techniques can be learned. The basic question is whether or not those of us concerned with the education of the young *want* to learn these skills and apply them consistently in our work. A related question involves whether the society in general, and educators in particular, want students to develop values haphazardly without any conscious and explicit involvement on the part of teachers. Or should students be helped explicitly to explore and come to some conclusions about values (both their own and those of other individuals in a wide variety of cultures)? It is my contention that explicitly helping students to explore and develop values is a legitimate goal for educators to pursue. Further, it is crucially important and badly needed in education today, and the *systematic* planning and design of school-wide instructional strategies is absolutely necessary to achieve it.

---

1. Are there any subjects that do not involve values in some way? If so, what are they?

2. Would you agree that students should be helped to explore and come to some conclusions about values in the classroom? Why or why not? Does your answer to this question depend in any way on the grade level of the children involved? Why or why not?

3. Should teachers discuss the values of students in class? Should students be encouraged to discuss the values of their teachers? Of the school administrators? Why or why not?

WHAT ARE VALUES?

A value is an idea—a concept—about what someone thinks is important in life. When a person values something, he or she deems it worthwhile—worth having, worth doing, or worth trying to obtain. The study of values usually is divided into the areas of aesthetics and ethics. *Aesthetics* refers to the study and justification of what human beings consider beautiful—what they enjoy. *Ethics* refers to the study and justification of conduct—how people behave. At the base of the study of ethics is the question of morals—the reflective consideration of what is right and wrong. Though some comments will be made about the teaching of aesthetic values in this book, our primary concern will be the teaching of ethics.

Like all ideas, values do not exist in the world of experience; they exist in people's minds. They are standards of conduct, beauty, efficiency, or worth that people endorse and that they try to live up to or maintain. All people have values, although they are not always consciously aware of what these values are.

As standards, values help us to determine—in the simplest sense— if we like something or not. In a more complex manner, values help us to determine whether a particular thing (an object, a person, an idea, a way of behaving, and so on) or class of things is good or bad.

The most important standards we have are the ones by which we judge conduct—by which we determine what kinds of actions are proper and worthwhile and what kinds are not. These standards are our *moral values*. Moral values represent guides to what is right and just. Thus a person may argue that it is right not to kill another person because human life is sacred. Since that person values human life, he considers the taking of a life wrong.

"I know it's a mess, but the real hidden beauty in homework like this is nobody will be able to copy it."

Source: *Today's Education*, NEA Journal, December 1972, p. 38.

MEANS AND ENDS

We often set certain standards to help us achieve or acquire other values. These are often called instrumental values. Instrumental values are the *means* people endorse as necessary and important in attaining other values, or *ends*. Thus a pianist may practice three hours every day without fail, because such practice will enable her to play the piano very well. Three hours' practice, in this instance is an instrumental value that will help this individual attain something else she considers important—being able to play the piano very well.

Do ends justify means? Is a father justified in stealing food to feed his hungry children? Are the police justified in breaking into people's homes in an effort to catch suspected drug pushers? Was the United States justified in dropping the atomic bomb on Hiroshima and Nagasaki to bring World War II to a close?

Ends can justify means. How else could they be justified? But this is not to say that any and all means are justified. The problem lies in determining whether *particular* ends justify *particular* means. Needless to say, this is often extremely difficult. A recurring danger lies in the fact that means can become so important to people that they become ends. This may or may not be a good thing. For example, some individuals, committed to the use of violence in wartime, may come to value it as the only way to resolve disputes and disagreements, even in peacetime. Some government leaders, committed to the rule of law as essential to the maintenance of law and order, may come to value laws for the sake of laws alone. Eventually they may insist that any law passed by the government be obeyed automatically, no matter what that law requires.

The reverse is also true. Ends may become so important to people that they fail to think about the propriety of the means necessary to achieve them. They decide to use any and all means at their disposal, no matter what they involve, to attain those ends. Perhaps the most tragic example of this in recent times was the murder of millions of Jews by the Nazis in death camps during World War II.

REASONS FOR VALUING [5]

The reasons people give for valuing things (a particular type of person, an object, a way of behaving) can tell us quite a bit about them. Certain foods, clothing, or types of music may be valued because they appeal to our tastes—because we find them pleasing to the senses. We feel good when we eat or wear or hear these things. Often we will go to a considerable amount of time or trouble to obtain or to be near them. Certain objects such as vintage wines, diamond rings, land at the seashore, or a government contract may be valued because they are worth (or may be-

[5] Jack R. Fraenkel, "Inquiry into Values," in Eugene Gilliom, ed., *Practical Methods for the Social Studies* (Belmont, Calif.: Wadsworth, 1977).

come worth) a large amount of money. Certain kinds of tools or appliances or materials may be valued because they work better than comparable others. Certain states of affairs or living conditions may be valued because they allow people to live in ways they otherwise could not. Some things may even be valued for no other reason than that the people who value them have been told they are worth valuing—that they are "important" or "worthwhile." Finally, certain ways of acting toward other human beings may be valued out of a deeply felt belief, based on experience and reflection, that these ways of acting are right and just.

---

1. Are some values better than others? If so, which ones? And how does one tell? (Look at this question from the reverse point of view as well. Are some values *worse* than others?)

2. What other reasons for valuing something can you suggest besides those suggested above?

VALUE CONFLICT

All people do not value the same things. The values of one person may be so different from those of another, in fact, that the two may find themselves in considerable disagreement, even conflict, with each other. The continuing controversy as to the value of capital punishment—the death penalty—as a deterrent to crime is a case in point. Those in favor of the death penalty argue that it will make potential murderers think twice. Those opposed to it argue that the crime rate in those states that employ capital punishment is no lower than the crime rate in the states that do not. Furthermore, they point out that taking an additional life will not replace the one that is gone.

Value conflict may not only be interpersonal (between individuals, as the above example suggests), but also intrapersonal—within one person. An individual may be torn between two or more conflicting desires or pressures to act in certain ways. Hunt and Metcalf, for example, describe a secretary who had developed a strong loyalty to her employer. He had provided her with good working conditions, raised her salary many times, given her several vacations, and even provided her with financial help for her aged mother. The secretary had recently discovered, however, that the employer had falsified his income tax returns. She thereupon sought advice from a local newspaper columnist as to what she should do. Should she remain loyal to her boss and keep her mouth shut? Or should she be honest and report him to the tax authorities? The secretary was faced with a conflict between two of her values—loyalty and honesty.[6]

---

[6] Maurice P. Hunt and Lawrence E. Metcalf, *Teaching High School Social Studies* (New York: Harper & Row, 1968), p. 124.

Chicago Tribune-New York News Syndicate, Inc.

1. What examples of value conflict can you cite that currently exist in the United States? What appears to be the primary cause of these conflicts? What do you think should be done to resolve each one?

2. Would you agree that "value conflict is a fact of life"? Why or why not?

3. Do you think any problems exist for which there are no solutions? If so, what might be an example of such a problem?

IDEAS AND FEELINGS

The more we can find out about what people value, the better, for in so doing we learn a lot about what makes them tick—the kinds of decisions they are likely to make, the leaders they will follow, the policies they will endorse, and the things on which they are likely to spend time, money, and energy. Indeed, it is virtually essential to study values if we are to learn and understand very much about a people—about their society, their culture, their art and music, their myths, their history, their ideas, their dreams, their goals.

Values are ideas about the worth of things; they are concepts, abstractions. As such, they can be defined, compared, contrasted, analyzed, generalized about, and debated. As standards, they can be used explicitly to judge the worth of things.

But values also have another dimension, an emotional one. For a value is a powerful emotional commitment, a strong liking for something. People care deeply about the things that they value. It is this fact—that values are both idea and feeling, that they have both cognitive and affective components—that so often is overlooked by many who profess to be "value educators" today.

If one accepts the definition of values as being both emotional commitments and ideas about worth, it follows logically that teachers interested in value education need to plan for both the emotional growth of students and the development of their intellectual abilities. Indeed, it can be argued that intellectual and emotional development are interdependent—that very much of one cannot take place without the other. As Beck writes,

Often we try to help a child understand a particular aspect of ethi-

cal theory; for example, we try to help him understand the need for reciprocal relationships (as in promise-keeping and formation of contracts); and we find that we fail, because there is a lack of sensitivity, a lack of concern, a lack of emotional development—a lack of *noncognitive* development which prevents him from having this cognitive insight. On the other hand, there are cases where we try to help a person become more sensitive to other people and their needs and more disposed to help them, and the (problem) is his lack of understanding of the place of concern for others in a person's life.[7]

Teachers who wish to engage in values education in any sort of comprehensive way, therefore, will need some procedures they can use to help students develop both intellectually and emotionally. This book suggests some of those procedures.

Chapter 2 discusses the nature of value indicators—what to look for in order to obtain some idea of what people value. Chapter 3 describes the approach to values education known as values clarification and discusses its strengths and weaknesses. Chapter 4 describes and discusses the "moral reasoning" approach that is based on the work of Lawrence Kohlberg and Jean Piaget. Chapter 5 then describes some additional ideas and strategies for teachers to consider that build on or go beyond the techniques described in Chapters 3 and 4. Last, Chapter 6 suggests a few skills that teachers will need to engage students in the procedures and strategies described in Chapters 3 through 5.

EXERCISES

1. Observe some teachers at work to see if they deal explicitly with value questions and issues in their classrooms. How many include discussions of values as a regular part of their classroom routine?

2. Interview a random number of adults on how they feel about values being discussed in the schools. How many are in favor? How many are opposed? Why are they in favor or opposed? Now interview a random number of people studying to be teachers. How many of this group are in favor of value discussions in schools? Opposed? Why are they in favor or opposed? What differences do you notice between the two groups? How would you explain these differences?

3. In April of 1976, a Gallup poll reported that an overwhelming

---

[7] Clive Beck, "The Development of Moral Judgment," in James A. Phillips, Jr., ed., *Developing Value Constructs in Schooling: Inquiry into Process and Product* (Worthington, Ohio: Ohio Association for Supervision and Curriculum Development, 1972), p. 44.

majority of the population favored instruction in morals and moral behavior in the public schools. The question the Gallup organization asked of those interviewed was as follows.

"Would you favor or oppose instruction in the schools that would deal with morals and moral behavior?"

	Favor	*Oppose*	*Don't Know*
National	79%	15%	6%
No children in school	76	17	7
Public school parents	84	12	4
Parochial school parents	85	13	2

The Gallup organization did not pursue this question further; that is, they did not attempt to determine how those people interviewed interpreted the term "instruction." Obviously, a number of interpretations are possible. Some people might consider "instruction in moral behavior" as simply telling children what adults believe is right and what is wrong. Others might think it means helping students to determine what is right and wrong for themselves. Both interpretations are fraught with difficulties, no matter which view (or some other one) one might endorse. What might some of these difficulties be? How would you define the phrase, "instruction in morals and moral behavior?" (Incidentally, is instruction in "morals" the same thing as instruction in "moral behavior"?)

4. As we have seen, values often conflict. In the United States, for example, some people urge that taller skyscrapers be built to save space, while others argue for lower buildings in order to maintain a view of the sky. Listed below are several things that at least some Americans value. Can you think of another value someone might hold that would conflict with each of those listed?

Value	*Opposing Value*
a. Lots more parking spaces.	
b. Freedom to do exactly as I want.	
c. Neighborhoods in which many different ethnic groups and races live.	
d. No noisy kids around.	
e. A city that is easy to walk around in.	
f. Lower school taxes.	
g. Eliminating air pollution.	
h. More and better sewage treatment.	

Value	*Opposing Value*

i. More parades to display civic pride.

j. More jobs for people who live in the city.

k. More green spaces within downtown city areas.

5. All societies prescribe as proper certain ideas, objects, and ways of behaving while they consider others improper. The ideas and behaviors considered proper, or "good," constitute the society's values. A wide gap often exists, however, between the values of a society and the daily life of the people in that society. In all societies there are individuals who act in ways that are contrary to those generally accepted as right. Values most often represent *ideal* behavior, not actuality. No society yet known completely fulfills the ideals it sets down as proper ways for its members to behave. Nonetheless, all societies do recognize the fact that each individual has a community of interest with the other members of the society and that certain actions are necessary and must be enforced if the society is to be preserved.

At first glance, this may seem difficult to believe in the case of the United States, which is made up of many different cultural streams and is characterized by rapid change. Detroit automobile tycoons, ghetto dwellers of our major cities, Philadelphia lawyers, Houston oilmen, Chicano lettuce pickers, and poor coal miners from the strip mines of Appalachia appear to be so different that America seems to defy description at times.

Nevertheless, many scholars have argued that through all of this diversity certain common threads do run. Though not all Americans believe in the same values, and even though many do not seem to practice what they do believe, certain broad unifying values can be identified. Here is one such list.

- Competitiveness for individual and material success (emphasis on personal, individual advancement).
- Equalitarianism (the belief that the possession of wealth, education, or reputation does not make one individual a better person than another).
- A tendency to provide moral or religious justifications for personal and national acts.
- A suspicion of authority.
- A strong reliance on common sense.
- An optimistic outlook toward life. (If a person works hard, can justify his or her actions morally, and uses good common sense, no task is impossible).

- Racism (not only outright prejudice and discrimination by many Whites against people of color, but also a pervasive assumption by most Whites that white is normal and black abnormal).
- A propensity toward violence as a means of solving problems.

Would you agree? Would most Americans support these values? Would you add or delete any from the list? Are these values *uniquely* American?

chapter two

VALUE INDICATORS

Values cannot be seen directly; they must be inferred from value indicators—what people say and do. Both the actions and statements of people offer clues about their values.

ACTIONS AS CLUES TO VALUES

People's actions often give us clues as to what they value. Try noticing what a person does with spare time when he or she is not being coaxed or threatened. Suppose, for example, that someone spends most of his free time tutoring children who are having trouble learning to read. The individual in this case spends a lot of time looking for suitable books and other materials that the children can use, finding quiet places to occupy while working with them, designing some special materials, and, of course, working with the children themselves. If the person is not required to do this and is not being paid for it we would be inclined to believe that he values this kind of activity. In other words, he considers tutoring an important and worthwhile thing to do.

Here are four examples of behavior. What values do they suggest?

Incident #1: A Book Burning

MINNEAPOLIS—Approximately three dozen copies of the novel, "Slaughterhouse Five," were burned in Drake, N.D., last week, on orders of the local school board.

Acting on the complaint of a sophomore student, the board held a special meeting on Tuesday, and agreed with the girl that the book was profane. Some ministers at the meeting described Kurt Vonnegut Jr.'s novel about the allied bombing of Dresden, Germany, in World War II as a "tool of the devil."

The board directed Dale Fuhrman, superintendent of schools, to supervise the books' destruction.

Other books scheduled to be destroyed because of allegedly profane language are "Deliverance" by James Dickey and an anthology of short stories by Ernest Hemingway, William Faulkner, and John Steinbeck.

All had been assigned to students of the central North Dakota town, population 700, by Bruce Severy, a 27-year-old English teacher who reportedly was hired because of his cosmopolitan outlook.

"All I can say is, the author is trying to tell his story like it is, using language as it is being used today out there in the real world," Severy said at the school board hearing.

Alluding to the fact that none of the school board members had read the books they ordered destroyed, Severy said, "No one can make a judgment about a book without reading the entire book. Anything less is academically dishonest, anti-intellectual and irrational."

The five-member board voted unanimously to burn the books and against rehiring Severy for next year.[1]

Incident #2: An Idealist Loses His Ideals

When I graduated from college I had plenty of ideals in honesty, fair play, and cooperation which I had acquired at home, in school, and from literature. My first job after graduation was selling typewriters. During the first day I learned that these machines were not sold at a uniform price but that a person who haggled and waited could get a machine at about half the list price. I felt that this was unfair to the customer who paid the list price. The other salesmen laughed at me and could not understand my silly attitude. They told me to forget the things I had learned in school, and that you couldn't earn a pile of money by being strictly honest. When I replied that money wasn't everything they mocked me: "Oh! No? Well, it helps." I had ideals and I resigned. . . .

It was quite a time before I could find another job. During this time I occasionally met some of my classmates and they related experiences similar to mine. They said they would starve if they were rigidly honest. All of them had girls and were looking forward to marriage and a comfortable standard of living, and they said they

---

[1] "Vonnegut Book Burned as 'Profane,'" *Chronicle* (San Francisco), November 12, 1973. © 1973 by The New York Times Company. Reprinted by permission.

did not see how they could afford to be rigidly honest. My own feelings became less determined than they had been when I quit my first job.

Then I got an opportunity in the used-car business. I learned that this business had more tricks for fleecing customers than [any] I had tried previously. Cars with cracked cylinders, with half the teeth missing from the flywheel, with everything wrong, were sold as "guaranteed." When the customer returned and demanded his guarantee, he had to sue to get it and very few went to that trouble and expense: the boss said you could depend on human nature. If hot cars could be taken in and sold safely, the boss did not hesitate. When I learned these things I did not quit as I had previously. I sometimes felt disgusted and wanted to quit, but I argued that I did not have much chance to find a legitimate firm. I knew that the game was rotten but it had to be played—the law of the jungle and that sort of thing. I knew that I was dishonest and to that extent felt that I was more honest than my fellows. The thing that struck me as strange was that all these people were proud of their ability to fleece customers. They boasted of their crookedness and were admired by their friends and enemies in proportion to their ability to get away with a crooked deal: it was called shrewdness. Another thing was that these people were unanimous in their denunciation of gangsters, robbers, burglars, and petty thieves. They never regarded themselves as in the same class and were bitterly indignant if accused of dishonesty: it was just good business.

Once in a while, as the years have passed, I have thought of myself as I was in college—idealistic, honest, and thoughtful of others— and have been momentarily ashamed of myself. Before long such memories became less and less frequent and it became difficult to distinguish me from my fellows. If you had accused me of dishonesty I would have denied the charge, but with slightly less vehemence than my fellow businessmen, for after all I had learned a different code of behavior.[2]

Incident #3: The Sailing of a Small Vessel

My friend Bill Huntington and I are planning to sail a small vessel westward into the Pacific H-bomb test area. . . . We will re-

[2] From *White Collar Crime* by Edward H. Sutherland. Copyright, 1949, by Holt, Rinehart and Winston, Inc. Reprinted by permission of Holt, Rinehart and Winston.

main there as long as the tests of H-bombs continue. . . . Why? Because it is the way I can say to my government, to the British government, and to the Kremlin: "Stop! Stop this madness before it is too late. For God's sake, turn back!"

I am going cause, as Shakespeare said, "Action is eloquence." Without some such direct action, ordinary citizens lack the power any longer to be seen or heard by their government.

I am going because it is time to *do something* about peace, not just *talk* about peace.

I am going because, like all men, in my heart I know that *all* nuclear explosions are monstrous, evil, unworthy of human beings.

I am going because war is no longer a feudal jousting match; it is an unthinkable catastrophe for all men.

I am going because it is now the little children, and, most of all, the as yet unborn who are the front line troops. It is my duty to stand between them and this horrible danger.

I am going because it is cowardly and degrading for me to stand by any longer, to consent, and thus to collaborate in atrocities.

I am going because, as Gandhi said, "God sits in the man opposite me: therefore to injure him is to injure God himself."

I am going to witness to the deep inward truth we all know, "Force can subdue, but love gains."

I am going because however mistaken, unrighteous, and unrepentant governments may seem, I still believe all men are really good at heart, and that my act will speak to them.

I am going in the hope of helping change the hearts and minds of men in government. If necessary I am willing to give my life to help change a policy of fear, force and destruction to one of trust, kindness, and help.

I am going in order to say, "Quit this waste, this arms race. Turn instead to a disarmament race. Stop competing for evil, compete for good."

I am going because I have to—if I am to call myself a human being.

When you see something horrible happening, your instinct is to do something about it. You can freeze in fearful apathy or you can even talk yourself into saying that it isn't too horrible. I can't do that. I have to act. This is too horrible. We know it. Let's all act.[3]

---

[3] Excerpted from Albert Bigelow, "Why I Am Sailing into the Pacific Bomb-Test Area," *Liberation*, February 1958. By permission of the publisher.

Incident #4: A Classroom Examination

Reprinted by permission of Newspaper Enterprise Association.

---

1. What do each of these incidents suggest about the values of the people involved?

2. What *actions* on the part of each of the individuals in the incidents presented could cause you to change your mind about what they value? Why?

3. What is the point of the cartoon on page 21? What does it have to do with values?

"Hector, let's play school. You be
the principal, and I'll be a teacher."

Source: *Today's Education*, December 1972, p. 27.

WORDS AS CLUES TO VALUES

Actions, therefore, are one clue to values. But a person's *words* can also provide some clues about what he or she values. Those words may appear in speeches, letters, proclamations, editorials, cartoons, articles, conversations, or other forms of written and/or spoken communication. Here are three examples of such statements. What do they say about the values of the authors?

Statement #1: The American Declaration of Independence

We hold these truths to be self-evident, that all Men are created equal, that they are endowed by their Creator with certain unalienable Rights, that among these are Life, Liberty, and the Pursuit of Happiness—That to secure these Rights, Governments are instituted among Men, deriving their just Powers from the Consent of the Governed—That whenever any Form of Government becomes destructive of these ends, it is the Right of the People to alter or to abolish it, and to institute new Government, laying its foundation on such principles and organizing its powers in such form, as to them shall seem most likely to effect their Safety and Happiness. Prudence, indeed, will dictate that Government long established should not be changed for light and transient causes; and accordingly all experience hath shewn, that mankind are more disposed to suffer, while evils are sufferable, than to right themselves by abolishing the forms to which they are accustomed. But when a long train of abuses and usurpations, pursuing invariably the same object evinces a design to reduce them under absolute Despotism, it is their right, it is their duty, to throw off such Government, and to provide new Guards for their future security.

Statement #2: An Excerpt form the Sermon on the Mount

Ye have heard that it hath been said, An eye for an eye, and a tooth for a tooth.

But I say unto you, That ye resist not evil; but whosoever shall smite thee on the right cheek, turn to him the other also.

Ye have heard that it hath been said, Thou shalt love thy neighbour, and hate thine enemy.

But I say unto you, Love your enemies, bless them that curse you, do good to them that hate you, and pray for them that despitefully use you, and persecute you (Matthew 19:38–39, 43–44).

Statement #3: An Argument for Morality

Man has developed admirable principles of morality, which in large part govern the actions of individual human beings. And yet, we are murderers, mass murderers. Almost all of us, even many of our religious leaders, accept with equanimity a world policy of devoting a large part of our world income, our world resources—one hundred billion dollars a year—to the cold-blooded readying of nuclear weapons to kill hundreds of millions of people, to damage the pool of human germ plasm in such a way that after a great nuclear war our descendants might be hardly recognizable as human beings.

Does the Commandment "Thou Shalt Not Kill" mean nothing to us? Are we to interpret it as meaning "Thou shall not kill except when the national leaders say to do so?"

I am an American, deeply interested in the welfare of my fellow Americans, of our great Nation. But I am first of all a human being. I believe in *morality*. Even if it were possible (which it is not) to purchase security for the United States of America by killing all of the hundreds of millions of people behind the Iron Curtain without doing any harm to anyone else, I would not be willing that it be done.

I believe that there is a greater power in the world than the evil power of military force, of nuclear bombs—there is the power of *good*, of *morality*, of *humanitarianism*.

I believe in the power of the human spirit. I should like to see our great Nation, the United States of America, take the lead in the fight for good, for peace, against the evil of war. I would like to see in our cabinet a Secretary for Peace, with a budget of billions of dollars per year, perhaps as much as 10 percent of the amount now expended for military purposes. I should like to see set up a great international research program involving thousands of scientists, economists, geographers, and other experts working steadily year after year in the search for possible solutions to world problems— ways to prevent war and to preserve peace.

During the past hundred years there have been astounding developments in science and technology, developments that have completely changed the nature of the world in which we live. So far as I can see, the nature of diplomacy, of the conduct of international affairs, has changed very little.

The time has now come for this aspect of the world to change, because we now recognize that the power to destroy the world is a power that cannot be used.

May our great nation, the United States of America, be the leader in bringing *morality* into its proper place of prime importance in the conduct of world affairs.[4]

Words, therefore, also can be value indicators. Such statements as those above, which indicate or imply that an individual or group considers a particular thing or group of things to have a certain amount of worth, merit, or quality (exactly how much is not always clear), are called *value judgments.*

What would you say is a better indicator of what a person values—what he or she says or does? Why?

TYPES OF VALUE JUDGMENTS

Value judgments appear in a variety of forms. More importantly, they have different meanings. For example, all the following statements are value judgments; yet they vary in terms both of intent and significance:

1. I prefer to attend the symphony rather than the ballet.
2. This painting is worth $1500 in hard cash from any professional art dealer in the country.
3. Democracy is the best form of government.
4. The United States should send food to nations where people are starving.

Some value judgments such as the statement, "I prefer to attend the symphony rather than the ballet," are no more than indications of personal preference or taste. The speaker is not trying to argue or suggest

---

[4] Linus Pauling, *No More War!* (New York: Dodd, Mead, 1958). Reprinted by permission of Dodd, Mead & Co.

that others should prefer this but is simply indicating what he likes himself.

Other value judgments such as the statement, "This painting is worth $1500 in hard cash from any art professional dealer in the country," are assertions that a particular object or type of object will bring a certain price in the marketplace of such objects. The speaker in this case is giving her estimate of what a certain group of people (art dealers) will pay at a particular time to obtain something that they desire (a particular painting). This value (the market value at a given time) may change over time. The amount that art dealers will pay for the painting may increase or decrease, but the speaker is not expressing merely a personal preference (though she *may* be doing that too). She is referring to the common opinion of a certain group of people as to what something is worth.

Some value judgments such as the statement, "Democracy is the best form of government," assert or imply that a certain thing is of greater worth or merit than are other similar and available alternatives, because it has more of the characteristics specified by a particular set of criteria (e.g., skill, energy, intelligence, strength, kindness, some combination of these, and so on).

Suppose, for example, that an employer remarks, "John is my best worker." When asked to explain the statement the employer replies, ". . . because he gets the most work done in the shortest time with the fewest number of mistakes." The employer is not merely expressing a personal preference; nor is he referring to the common opinion of a group of people as to what something is worth. He is asserting that a particular worker, John, is better than other workers, because John outperforms them in terms of a certain set of applicable criteria (amount of work done, speed, number of mistakes).

Finally, other value judgments such as the statement, "The United States should send food to nations where people are starving," are prescriptions of policy. They indicate what the speaker thinks should be done in one or more instances in order to achieve desired consequences.[5]

When a person states that such-and-such is better than so-and-so *because* it possesses certain characteristics or *because* this or that will result, we can check out the facts involved and see if what the person says is true. That is, we can confirm whether or not the person or object in question does possess the characteristics stated and whether or not the stated consequences have resulted from similar actions or policies in the past. This doesn't make the item referred to "better" in any absolute or final sense, but it does tell us why the person thinks it is better. People

---

[5] When issued by politicians or government decision makers, this type of value judgment usually is called a *policy statement*.

using a different set of criteria might come to quite a different conclusion.

It might be helpful at this point to say a few words about a point of confusion that exists among value educators today. This is the so-called distinction between factual judgments and value judgments. The argument in support of this distinction goes something like this: Factual judgments are assertions made about the observable world and things that exist or take place within it. Such judgments can be highly specific as to time, place, and individuals involved. For example: The formal surrender of Japan that signaled the end of World War II took place on September 2, 1945, aboard the U.S.S. *Missouri.* Or, such judgments can be very general: When an inconsistent or unusual object is inserted into a sequence of objects a viewer's attention, curiosity, and interest as to those objects increase. But factual judgments have one basic characteristic in common. They are ultimately testable by recourse to observation. Value judgments, on the other hand, rate or evaluate certain aspects of experience or prescribe certain courses of action.

Reflection suggests that the distinction does not hold, however, or at best, holds only in part. Some value judgments *are* factual judgments. Take statement #2 above, for example. The speaker is not only saying what she thinks a particular painting is worth but is also making a statement of fact that can be checked out easily by a quick trip to a professional art dealer. Or consider statement #1. When a person states that he prefers to attend the symphony rather than the ballet, he is telling us something about his behavior that we can observe easily.

Other value judgments *become* factual judgments as soon as their meaning is explored. Once we know what statement #3's speaker means by the term "best" we can determine if the statement holds up or not *according to that definition* (which is all we can do for any statement). Policy statements, like #4 above, are made for a reason—because the speaker believes that certain consequences will result. It is a question of *fact* as to whether or not such consequences indeed will occur. Our estimate of the likelihood of their occurrence can help us to determine if we should or should not put the policy into operation.

Students, like the rest of us, are frequently exposed to value judgments. That teaching them to recognize such judgments will be to their benefit seems only logical, for it will make them aware of the fact that value judgments are usually made for a reason. By helping them to seek out and assess these reasons, we can help students to determine whether the judgments are those that they themselves would make.

Both a person's words and actions, therefore, may constitute *evidence* of what he or she values. We cannot be absolutely sure, of course, since the person may be trying to deceive or confuse us. Thus, the more evidence we have (the more of a person's actions and sayings we have

Source: San Francisco *Chronicle*, September 7, 1975. © King Features Syndicate, Inc. 1975.

observed under a variety of conditions), the more accurate a picture we are likely to obtain of what that person values.

1. Here are a number of value judgments. How would you go about trying to support or refute them? Is it possible to "prove the truth" of these judgments in any way?

   a. Bob Thomas likes to play chess better than any other game you can name.

   b. That chair is an excellent piece of work.

   c. 1965 Chevrolets in good condition will bring more money in the used-car market than 1965 Fords.

   d. Dwight Eisenhower was a much better president than Harry Truman.

   e. A used, Gitane, 10-speed bicycle is worth more than a used Schwinn of the same year and in similar condition.

   f. Alice Stevenson loves the symphony.

   g. Rock is better music than that Big Band stuff of the 1930s.

   h. The most valuable man a college basketball team can have is a high-scoring center who is aggressive and at least seven feet tall.

   i. Brand X refrigerators are not as good as Brand Y refrigerators.

   j. Mrs. Adams is the best teacher in the school.

   k. The death penalty should be abolished.

   l. Marilyn is a very beautiful woman.

2. Would it be possible for the real (i.e., "true") value of something to be greater or lesser than its cost or price at a given time? If so, can you think of any examples of such items?

DEGREES OF VALUE

Are some values more important than others? Are there any values that all people endorse? Moral absolutists, for instance, argue that there are "eternal values" somewhere in the cosmos that are by their very nature "desirable" to possess. Such values, they say, are absolute. They apply everywhere and always have. They identify certain human actions that are *always* right or *always* wrong, regardless of circumstance. "There are certain human acts which are of their very nature, that is, intrinsically, bad and deserving of blame." [6]

At first glance, this seems a reasonable position. After all, are there not many patterns of human conduct—such as helping others in need and being fair—that are universally held to be good? And, on the other hand, are there not certain practices such as murder and torture that all people would condemn?

The problem here lies in the nature of the word "absolute"; for absolutes, by definition, allow of no exceptions or conditions. For a pattern of behavior to qualify as a moral absolute, it must hold in every circumstance or situation in which human beings might be involved. If even one exception can be justified, the pattern loses its claim to absolute status. And no one has ever come up with a pattern of behavior for which some justifiable exception has not been found.

In contradistinction to moral absolutism is moral relativism. Moral relativists believe that there is a plurality of value positions people can take and that any one value is no more important, or "better," than any other. Although he is not a relativist himself, W. T. Stace provides us with an extremely clear description of the relativist viewpoint.

> The whole notion of progress is a sheer delusion. Progress means an advance from lower to higher, from worse to better. But on the basis of ethical relativity, it has no meaning to say that the standards of this age are better (or worse) than those of the previous age. For there is no common standard by which both can be measured. Thus it is nonsense to say that the morality of the New Testament is higher than that of the Old. And Jesus Christ, if he imagined that he was introducing into the world a higher ethical standard than existed before his time, was merely deluded.
>
> On this view, Jesus Christ can only have been led to the quite

---

[6] William McGucken, "The Philosophy of Catholic Education," in N. B. Henry, ed., *Philosophies of Education*, Forty-first Yearbook of the National Society for the Study of Education. (Chicago: The Society, 1942), p. 254.

absurd belief that his ethical precepts were better than those of Moses by his personal vanity. If only he had read Dewey, he would have understood that so long as people continued to believe in the doctrine of an eye for an eye and a tooth for a tooth, that doctrine was morally right; and that there could not be any point whatever in trying to make them believe in his newfangled theory of loving one's enemies. Too, the new morality would become right as soon as people came to believe in it, for it would then be the accepted standard. And what people think is right is right. But then if only Jesus Christ and persons with similar ideas had kept these ideas to themselves, people might have gone on believing that the old morality was right. And in that case, it would have been right, and would have remained so to this day. And that would have saved a lot of useless trouble. For the change which Jesus Christ actually brought about was merely a change from one set of moral ideas to another.[7]

Relativists leave us with the impression that value judgments are no more than expressions of taste, of what one person prefers but another does not. They appear to suggest that all disagreements about values boil down to differences in terms of what people like and hence, that such disagreements cannot be resolved. "You have your likes and dislikes, and I have mine. While I may not agree with your preferences or you with mine, you are certainly entitled to yours, just as I am entitled to mine." This is a common attitude when disagreements over questions of value arise.

Now there is indeed some truth in the above statement. All value judgments are *at the very least* statements of preference; *some* value judgments, as we have seen, may be *only* statements of preference. But many are intended to convey more than just that; in many instances a person means to indicate something more than just what he or she likes or dislikes. A value judgment may be meant to indicate what a certain group of people thinks something is worth, for example. Or it may be meant to argue that something is superior to its alternatives in certain ways or to prescribe a particular course of action.

The above comments lead us into the argument of logical positivists. Positivists argue that only judgments of fact (factual judgments) can be verified but that judgments of value (value judgments) cannot. Factual judgments, as we have seen, are statements about things that actually exist or that have happened in the past, are happening, or will happen in the future. They include the activities of individuals, the locations of places, the dates of events, the sizes of objects. Such statements provide

---

[7] W. T. Stace, *The Concept of Morals* (New York: Copyright 1937 by Macmillan Publishing Co., Inc., renewed 1965 by Walter T. Stace), pp. 48–49.

us with information about people, things, and events and can be checked out as true or false by anyone interested in doing so through observation and research.

Judgments of value, so the positivists claim, cannot be tested publicly, for they deal with feelings and inclinations and include such value terms as "good," "beautiful," "desirable," and so on. Such statements do not say something about the world as it is but as we would like it to be. They are not open to verification through observation and experiment.

Positivists, however, appear to overlook the fact that statements of value *can* be submitted to public test if we can come to some agreement on the value term or terms involved. The statements that Brand X is a "better" automobile than Brand Y or that Michael is a "better" teacher than Dolores are testable enough if those concerned with automobiles or teachers can agree on the meaning of the value term involved. (In these examples, the value term is "better.") Obtaining such agreement, of course, is not always an easy matter, but there are ways to go about it.

Finally, it is evident that people *do* attach more importance to some values than they do to others, though not everyone is agreed as to which values are the more important ones. As I mentioned earlier, some values such as a liking for chocolate rather than vanilla ice cream or rock over country-and-western music are essentially personal preferences. They represent an individual's personal taste—what he or she likes better than other things of a similar nature. People are not likely to argue that other people also should value such things, though they usually are rather pleased if they do. A person's taste also depends on his experiences. One's taste is likely to be rather narrow until one has had opportunities to experience many different kinds of things. In the process, one becomes aware of *alternatives*—aware that there are many different kinds of things to have and to do that *can* be enjoyed and perhaps valued. It is because of this that teachers should try to engage students in as many different experiences as possible—to broaden their awareness of what the world has to offer.

There are other values, however, that many people consider far more important than personal preferences in the world's affairs. Such values, in fact, are considered of such importance that people often do argue that other people also should hold them. World peace is such a value for many people; human dignity, another; equal opportunity, a third; happiness, a fourth. They are held as essential to the maintenance of life in general and to the quality of life in particular. Many other values such as honesty, cleanliness, tact, or bravery, fall someplace in between these extremes.[8] Most of us are unlikely to argue that these values are essential to the

[8] James P. Shaver and William Strong, *Facing Value Decisions: Rationale-Building for Teachers* (Belmont, Calif.: Wadsworth Publishing Co., 1976).

"Telephone, Harold. A Mr. Smith from the Environmental
Protection Agency would like a word with you."

Source: San Francisco *Sunday Chronicle-Examiner,* "This World" section, July 22, 1973.
Reprinted by permission of Newspaper Enterprise Association.

survival of the species. Yet we do consider them more important than personal preferences. And a value that at one time is essentially a personal
preference may take on the status of a more basic, fundamental value over
time or in certain contexts. The value now placed on ecology—developing
and maintaining a clean and healthy environment—is an example.

---

1. Suppose you were asked to name three values that you think most Americans would endorse. What would you name?

2. Are there any values that you think most people throughout the *world*
would endorse? If so, what are they?

3. What values do you think are most important? Why? Would you argue that
other people should also hold these values? Why or why not?

4. Are there values you endorse that your parents do not, or vice versa? If
so, how would you explain this?

EXERCISES

1. Locate some newspaper and/or magazine articles containing statements that you feel have value implications. Show them to some of your
friends or classmates, and ask them what values they think the articles

reflect. To what extent do their viewpoints coincide with yours? How would you explain any differences in viewpoints?

2. Keep a record over a period of time of a public figure's statements that you believe have value implications. How consistent is he or she? What, if anything, does consistency have to do with values?

3. It is often said that we can tell what a person values by observing how he or she acts. Would the converse also be true? Can we tell what a person does *not* value by observing his or her actions? Why or why not?

4. Listed below are a number of value judgments. What values would you say each of these statements reflects?

   a. Students should be taught *how* to think, not *what* to think.
   b. All students should be assigned a minimum of eight hours of homework per week.
   c. Talking above a whisper should not be permitted in the library.
   d. The length of a male student's hair should not be permitted to extend beneath the top of his shirt collar.
   e. All students should be required to wear shoes to class.
   f. Social studies teachers should use a variety of source material in their teaching rather than just a single textbook.
   g. No textbook should be used in the public schools that does not deal with the contributions of minority groups and women to American life.
   h. Students should be encouraged to design their own experiments and projects in science classes.
   i. Compositions should be written in ink.
   j. Teachers should concentrate on teaching concepts and important ideas rather than having students memorize a lot of unrelated facts.

5. Listed below are a number of values that various people have identified as important to them. Pick the three most important and the three least important as far as you are concerned. Compare your selections with those of other individuals. What differences do you notice? Similarities? How would you explain these differences and similarities? Are there any of these (or other) values that you think should be taught directly in school? Why or why not?

honesty	hard work	survival
politeness	love of country	sanctity of life
cleanliness	freedom of speech	trial by a jury of one's peers
justice	freedom of assembly	freedom from unreasonable
courage	freedom of worship	searches and seizures
a speedy trial	freedom from cruel and unusual punishment	
punctuality		

chapter three

VALUES CLARIFICATION

One of the most widely used approaches to values education in schools today is the values clarification approach espoused by Raths, Harmin, and Simon in their book, *Values and Teaching*.[1] Raths and his colleagues concern themselves more with the *process* of valuing than with the nature of values themselves. They state that values are based on three processes: choosing, prizing, and acting. Accordingly, they define a value as that which results when all seven of the criteria below are satisfied.

Choosing: (1) freely
            (2) from alternatives
            (3) after thoughtful consideration of the consequences of each alternative
Prizing: (4) cherishing, being happy with the choice
            (5) willing to affirm the choice publicly
Acting: (6) doing something with the choice
            (7) repeatedly, in some pattern of life [2]

Collectively, these seven processes are what the authors mean by *valuing*. The results that emerge when *all* seven of the processes are employed represent values to Raths, Harmin, and Simon. They then present a variety of "strategies" (more like activities or techniques) that teachers can use to engage students in one or more of the processes. Because of the widespread popularity of values clarification and the ease of the activities, even for those with only a minimum of training, we will examine

---

[1] Louis E. Raths, Merrill Harmin, and Sidney B. Simon, *Values and Teaching* (Columbus, Ohio: Charles E. Merrill Publishing Co., 1966). By permission of Charles E. Merrill Publishing Co.
[2] Ibid., p. 30.

the approach in some detail in this chapter. To give you a feeling for what the approach involves, we will take a look at a number of the kinds of activities that values clarifiers recommend. Some of the strengths and weaknesses of the approach will then be identified and discussed.

THE CLARIFYING RESPONSE

The basic or key technique involved in values clarification involves what Raths calls a *clarifying response*—a way of responding to things that students say or do to get them to reflect on what they have chosen, on what they prize, or on the kinds of things they are doing in life. But let Raths and his associates speak for themselves:

> Here is [an] actual situation. In this incident the clarifying response prods the student to clarify his thinking and to examine his behavior to see if it is consistent with his ideas. It is between lessons and a student has just told a teacher that science is his favorite subject.
> *Teacher:* What exactly do you like about science?
> *Student:* Specifically? Let me see. Gosh, I'm not sure. I guess I just like it in general.
> *Teacher:* Do you do anything outside of school to have fun with science?
> *Student:* No, not really.
> *Teacher:* Thank you, Jim. I must get back to work now.
> Notice the brevity of the exchanges. . . . An extended series of probes might give the student the feeling that he was being cross-examined and might make him defensive. Besides, it would give him too much to think about. The idea is, without moralizing, to raise a few questions, leave them hanging in the air, and then move on. The student to whom the questions are addressed, and other students who might overhear, may well ponder the question later, in a lull in the day or in the quiet moments before falling asleep. Gentle prods, but the effect is to stimulate a student who is ready for it to choose, prize, and act in ways outlined by the value theory.[3]

The primary intent of a clarifying response is to get students to look more closely at their behavior and ideas, thereby "clarifying" for themselves what they really value. Moralizing is to be deliberately avoided.

---

1. "The primary intent of a clarifying response is to get students to look more closely at their behavior and ideas. . . ." Do you think it does this? Why or why not?

[3] Ibid., p. 55.

2. Values clarifiers stress the fact that moralizing (indicating to students what the teacher thinks is right or wrong) is to be deliberately avoided in using a clarifying response. Would you agree that this is important? Why or why not? Can you think of any times when a person might deliberately *want* to moralize? If so, when?

3. Could a clarifying response ever be harmful? If so, how?

VALUE SHEETS

A value sheet is a thought-provoking story, statement, or set of questions containing value implications for students to reflect on and write or talk about. Some examples follow.

Louis Armstrong and his Art [4]

"I don't want a million dollars. See what I mean? No medals. I mean, I don't feel no different about the horn now than I did when I was playin' in the Tuxedo Band. That my livin' and my life. I love them notes. That why I try to make 'em right. See? And any part of the day, you liable to see me doing something toward it for the night.

"A lot of musicians, money make a damn fool out of them. They forget all about the life they love, standin' on the bandstand. They get famous and can't play no louder or no softer, and I ain't goin' play no less. I might play a little *more,* but always up to par." Some questions:

   a. Underline the places where Louis Armstrong tells you what he feels about art.
   b. Circle the statements which he uses to describe "other" artists.
   c. Is there anything you do which you are as dedicated to as Mr. Armstrong is about his trumpet playing?
   d. How does one go about beginning to care that deeply?

A Student's Report of a Campus Incident [5]

Someone was caught cheating on an exam in an advanced biology class. The teacher tried to take the paper away, but the boy held on to it. When the teacher finally got hold of the test, several index cards fell out from between the pages. The boy screamed that they were not his. To make a long story short, the teacher informed the student that this would have to be reported to the authorities. The boy threatened to kill the teacher, and they scuffled until other teachers came to get the boy away. The boy had been accepted by a

---

4 Ibid., pp. 104, 231.
5 Ibid., p. 241.

medical school, and this incident meant no med school for him. His actions were explained by a weak personality cracking under the system. But what amazed me was the reactions of the other pre-med students. Their near joy was hard to hide. How awfully sadistic. Or was their joy a sign of relief for not having been caught themselves? To think on:

1. What is your first, most immediate reaction? (Use free association. Don't write sentences; just put down words.)
2. In what ways do you identify with the boy?
3. In what ways do you identify with the teacher?
4. The author of the incident raises a point about the other students in the class. Comment on that.
5. To cheat or not to cheat? What is the rationalization for each position?
6. What alternatives were open to the student? to the teacher? to the other students?

Friendship [6]

1. What does friendship mean to you?
2. If you have friends, did you choose them or did they get to be your friends by accident?
3. In what ways do *you* show friendship?
4. How important do you think it is to develop and maintain friendships?
5. If you plan to make any changes in your ways, please say what changes you will make. If you do not intend to make any changes in your ways, write "No changes."

RANK-ORDERING

This technique asks students to differentiate among possible alternatives in terms of relative goodness and badness and to examine and clarify their preferences in terms of priorities. The choices presented to students can range from the very simple to the most complex, from very trivial kinds of concerns to those of considerable significance. Consider some simple examples first:

- Number in order the places in the list below that you would like to visit: _____ Mexico _____ New Zealand _____ the Soviet Union _____ China _____ England _____ Brazil _____ the Philippines _____ Israel _____ Egypt.

[6] Ibid., p. 95.

- Which of the following would you least like to do?
  - _____ Attend a ballet.
  - _____ Attend a symphony.
  - _____ Attend a baseball game.
  - _____ Attend a rock concert.
  - _____ Attend the theatre.
- Which of the following do you think is most important?
  - _____ A lot of friends.
  - _____ A lot of money.
  - _____ A lot of possessions.
  - _____ A lot of intelligence.
  - _____ A lot of curiosity.
  - _____ A lot of strength.

A more complex example, for use with older students, follows.

Church, State, and Political Agent [7]

Although you live in a small, rather conservative community (population of 5,000), you like to think of yourself as an open-minded, liberal sort of person. And, in fact, everyone is impressed with the way you pick up new ideas and follow current fads. Most everyone is aware that you have taken part in various civil rights and peace demonstrations and are committed to the need for reforms in various segments of American society. Last year, in a burst of community spirit, you joined several civic clubs, the volunteer fire department, the PTA, and a well-established, prominent religious group. Like most people, you haven't thought much about religion and are rather uncomfortable when it is being discussed, but if someone pinned you down, the following statements would be characteristic of your beliefs:

- All religions are based on the worship of a higher power.
- Any religion is all right as long as it doesn't interfere with someone else's right to worship as he sees fit.
- Freedom of religion is one of the great guarantees of the Constitution.
- A man with some kind of religion is better than a man with no religion at all.

One night a town meeting is called to discuss an immediate problem. The American Church of Satan has purchased an old house on the edge of the city and plans to use it as a "house of worship" and a center for teaching white magic and mystic arts. Although no one will admit it, there is an atmosphere of fear and panic.

[7] J. Doyle Casteel and Robert J. Stahl, *Value Clarification in the Classroom: A Primer* (Pacific Palisades, Calif.: Goodyear Publishing Co., 1975), pp. 79–80. Copyright 1975 by Goodyear Publishing Company. Reprinted by permission.

After a lengthy discussion in which many views are expressed, several possible ways of dealing with the situation are advanced:

1. Pass a zoning ordinance, retroactive to the previous year, that would prohibit using the location of the old house for a public meeting place but that would also stop construction of a new movie theatre down the block.
2. Simply tell the American Church of Satan that it is unwelcome in the community and give members a deadline for leaving, after which they will be arrested for trespassing.
3. Do nothing about the church because they have as much right as any religious group to be in town.
4. Do nothing, but ask the police to watch the house closely to make sure nothing illegal or immoral is occurring.
5. Ask the group to appear before a town meeting and to explain their beliefs and practices; then decide what to do.
6. Ask the church to deposit $10,000 in a local bank as an insurance against possible damage to the city or its inhabitants.

The mayor then asks you to prepare a leaflet in which you rank the proposals in order, from the best solution to the worst. Although you are pleased to do so, you are worried because you had planned to run for public office, and how you handle this assignment may well determine whether or not the community will support you.

In keeping with my beliefs I rank the proposals as follows:

_____ Proposal 1: Zoning Ordinance.
_____ Proposal 2: Ask to Leave.
_____ Proposal 3: Leave Alone.
_____ Proposal 4: Police Supervision.
_____ Proposal 5: Appear at Town Meeting.
_____ Proposal 6: Security Deposit.

I selected proposal _____ as best because _____

_____.

I Selected proposal _____ as worst because _____

_____.

Discussion Starters

1. Describe the nature of the problem this situation requires you to resolve.
2. What is the difference between the best solution and the worst solution?
3. Assuming the situation were true, how would you feel about being the person who had to make this decision? Why?

4. Do you consider yourself to be a liberal or conservative? Why? What are you according to this worksheet?

5. In view of this exercise, do you think you can say you favor freedom of religion, in the broadest sense of the phrase? Explain your answer.

---

1. Are there any topics on which value sheets should not be written? If so, what are they?

2. Some critics of values clarification have argued that the questions students are asked about value sheets or in rank-order exercises influence them to respond in certain ways. The result is that these exercises really focus more on the values of the question-asker than on those of the students participating in the exercise. Take a look at the questions following the value sheets and in the rank-order exercises presented above. Do they tend to support or refute this criticism?

THE PUBLIC INTERVIEW

The public interview is an activity in which student volunteers are publicly queried about some of their beliefs, feelings, and actions. Raths and his colleagues describe the procedures involved.[8]

One of the more dramatic value techniques is called the public interview. Let's look at one which took place in an elementary school class and see how it develops.

Teacher: Today, class, I would like to introduce the public interview. For this we need a volunteer, someone willing to be interviewed publicly, in front of the whole class.

The person interviewed comes up and sits here at my desk, in front of the room. I will go to his seat and interview him from there. The spotlight, you see, is on the person being interviewed.

Now, what I will do first is ask what topic the interviewee wants to talk about. He can choose one of the topics on our list of value areas,* or any other topic, even a very particular topic, like what he did over the weekend, or an idea he has, or a problem or decision he is facing. Anything he chooses.

Then I will ask him clarifying questions, questions that may help *him* get clearer on the topic of the interview, or questions that I think may help the class to get clearer on what he is saying.

---

[8] Raths, Harmin, and Simon, *Values and Teaching*, pp. 142–144.
* On the wall may be posted a list of significant value areas, such as friendship, use of time, use of money, love, morals, freedom, responsibility, politics, occupational choice, family, etc.

By the way, if you volunteer and pick "smorgasbord," then I choose the topic. You can always veto my choice, however.

And if you volunteer, relax, you always have an "out." If I ask you any question that is too personal or that you would rather not answer here in front of everyone, you just say, "I pass," and I will go right on to another question.

And if you want to end the interview, you just say, "Thank you for your questions." That's the signal for you to take your own seat and for the interview to terminate. . . .

Now who will be the first to take the interview seat? . . .

All right, Paul, you be the first. Others may have a chance another time. Take my seat, Paul. I'll sit in the back. How do you feel, Paul?

Paul: (In the teacher's chair) O.K., I guess.

Teacher: Do you recall what you say if you would rather not answer a particular question? (Making certain the safeguards are understood.)

Paul: I pass.

Teacher: And if you want to end the interview before time runs out?

Paul: I say, "Thank you for your questions."

Teacher: Fine, Paul, now on what topic would you like to be interviewed?

Paul: My sister.

Teacher: Would you care to tell us something about your sister, Paul?

Paul: Not especially. Except that we hate each other. I want to be interviewed, asked questions, rather than just to say something.

Teacher: O.K., Paul. What do you hate about your sister?

Paul: Well, she is two years younger than I am, and she always is in the way. Like she argues about what TV program to watch, and she hangs around me when I'm playing, and she . . . she is just a nuisance.

Teacher: Are there some times when you *like* having her around?

Paul: No, absolutely not. (Laughter.)

Teacher: How do you define hate? What do you mean by that word?

Paul: Terrible. Like I want to murder her. She should go away.

Teacher: What's the difference between hate and dislike?

Paul: One is stronger. Hate is stronger.

Teacher: What is the difference between hating someone and hating things that the person does?

Paul: Hmmm. I just thought of a time when I didn't hate my sister. Once we were walking along and someone said how nice we looked together, we were younger and were walking hand in hand. It was a good feeling. But, I don't know if you hate enough things a person does I guess you end up hating the person. Is that right?

Teacher: What do you think?

Paul: I don't know.

Teacher: Paul, what are you going to do about the situation between you and your sister? Apparently you don't like things the way they are.

Paul: What can I do? I know what I'd *like* to do . . . (Laughter.)

Teacher: Well, one thing you can do is keep away from her. Another is to try to work things out so that there is less argument and conflict between you. What other alternatives are there?

Paul: I don't know. I don't know. But thank you for your questions. Can I go now?

Teacher: Certainly, Paul, that's the rule. Whenever you want. Thank you. . . .

---

1. The questions that may be asked in a public interview are of considerable variety. For example, Simon and his associates [9] have suggested the following questions, among others, that could be asked of older children: "Do you believe in God?" "Are you likely to marry out of your race?" "Would you invite a black person to your house for dinner?" "Do you go to Sunday school or religion class?" and "What do you think of a mother who slaps her small son's hand for playing with his genitals?"

   a. Do you think such questions are appropriate? Why or why not?

   b. Are there any subjects that children should *not* be publicly questioned about? If so, what are they? Why shouldn't they be questioned about these topics?

2. One of the major arguments that values clarifiers make for the public interview is that students will "inevitably" review their answers mentally and thoughtfully consider what they have said in their public statements.[10] Would you agree that this is likely to happen? Why or why not?

3. Would you use this activity yourself? Why or why not?

VALUES VOTING

In this activity, a teacher reads questions aloud, one by one. Each question begins with the words, "How many of you . . . ?" For example, "How many of you like to go on long walks or hikes?" After each question is read the students take a position by a show of hands. Those in the affirmative raise their hands; those in the negative point their thumbs

9 Sidney B. Simon, Leland W. Howe, and Howard Kirschenbaum, *Values Clarification: A Handbook of Practical Strategies for Teachers and Students* (New York: Hart Publishing Co., 1972), pp. 140–146, passim.

10 Ibid., p. 139.

down, while those who are undecided fold their arms. Those who want to pass do nothing. Discussion is tabled until the teacher has completed the entire list of questions.

The sorts of questions in values voting range from the innocuous (e.g., "How many of you would like to be a teacher? A nurse? In politics?"), to the quite sensitive (e.g., "How many of you could tell someone they have bad breath?"), to those with moral implications (e.g., "How many of you think there are times when cheating is justified?")

Should students be encouraged to vote on value questions? Why or why not?

THE VALUE CONTINUUM

This exercise asks students to indicate where they stand on a particular issue or topic by marking their positions on a line that extends from one extreme to the other vis à vis the issue. Students later are asked to share their reasons for their positions with the rest of the class if they wish, or they may pass. Some examples follow.[11]

· How much do you talk to other people?

Tight-Lipped Tommy :   :   :   :   Blabber-Mouth Bertha

· How do you feel about divorce?

Steadfast Stella—   :   :   :   :   Multi-Marrying Martha—
Under no circum-   At the drop of the first un-
stances.   kind word.

· How do you feel about integration?

             :   :   :   :   :   :

Favor complete and   Compulsive moderate.   Actively opposed.
immediate integration.   Fights for open housing   Withdraws child from
Enforced busing.   except in own neighbor-   public school.
                              hood.

· How do you like teachers to relate to you?

             :   :   :   :   :   :

Super-Buddy—Let's us   Compulsive moderate.   Very strict and punitive.
do anything.   Yells constantly, but   Beats us for a grammar
                      doesn't do anything to   error.
                      stop us.

· What percentage of the time are you happy?

Sad-Sack Sara 0   :   :   :   : 100   Happy-Time Helen

· How much do you try to please the teacher?

Rebel Ralph :   :   :   :   :   Apple Polisher Al

11 Ibid., pp. 122–123.

EITHER-OR CHOICES

Students are presented with two alternatives and asked to choose between them, expressing their choice orally or in writing. Those with opposing choices then are paired off or grouped for discussion of the reasons behind their differences. Some illustrations of the kinds of questions in this activity follow.[12]

Is your favorite vacation place in the mountains or on the seashore?
Should the city council increase or decrease spending on recreation?
Should school attendance be required or not required?
Should ecology or energy be given top priority?
Was President Truman more of a statesman or a politician?
Should we increase or decrease contacts with China?

---

1. Value continua and either-or choices ask students to identify where they stand on a particular issue, but they do not require them to justify their positions. Is this appropriate? Should students be required to justify their positions on various issues? Why or why not?

2. Does a teacher ever have the right to question a student's stand on an issue? If so, when?

CRITIQUE

There is little question that values clarification has had a considerable impact on many teachers, teacher trainers, and curriculum developers. Conferences, workshops, articles, and books dealing with the approach have proliferated.[13] Many of the activities and techniques developed by values clarifiers are both interesting and useful in helping and encouraging students to think about their own personal commitments. They are

---

[12] John U. Michaelis, *Social Studies for Children in a Democracy*, 6th ed. (Englewood Cliffs, N.J., Prentice-Hall, Inc., 1976), p. 245.

[13] For example, in addition to the basic, original work by Raths, Harmin, and Simon, *Values and Teaching*, see Simon, Howe, and Kirschenbaum, *Values Clarification: A Handbook of Practical Strategies for Teachers and Students* (New York: Hart Publishing Co., 1972); Merrill Harmin, Howard Kirschenbaum, and Sidney B. Simon, *Clarifying Values Through Subject Matter: Applications for the Classroom* (Minneapolis: Winston Press, 1973); Leland W. Howe and Mary Martha Howe, *Personalizing Education: Values Clarification and Beyond* (New York: Hart Publishing Co., 1975). *Readings in Values Clarification*, edited by Howard Kirschenbaum and Sidney B. Simons, contains many articles written by those who endorse the values clarification approach (Minneapolis: Winston Press, 1973).

easy to master and fun to use. The clarifying response in particular has much to recommend it as a technique for use in values education. It avoids preaching, is accepting of student ideas, and encourages students to think about alternatives. The basic relativism underlying values clarification as a whole, however, is open to serious criticism, as are some of the activities developed to promote choosing, prizing, and acting. An examination of some of these weaknesses comes next.

Many authors writing about values clarification stress the "value theory" supposedly underlying the approach. Indeed, Raths and his associates state that *Values and Teaching* outlines a theory of values upon which their approach is based. Upon closer examination, however, one finds little that might legitimately be called a "theory." Most values clarification authors, in fact, simply suggest a number of activities that teachers can use to help students clarify their own personal commitments. A *theory* is a set of interrelated propositions suggesting various relationships believed to exist in the real world. This set of propositions can be supported or refuted by recourse to observable evidence. The strength of a theory lies in its capability to explain why things happen and to predict phenomena. One searches in vain, however, for such a set of propositions in the values clarification literature. At best, one finds only a few assumptions by authors as to *how* values develop. These assumptions do not in any way help to explain *why* they develop this way. Nor do the assumptions predict how individuals with certain values are likely to act in a given situation. They don't tell what to do when values conflict or even how—or if—the holding of a *particular* value affects the development of other values. All these are considerations one might reasonably expect a theory of values to provide some ideas about.

A second criticism is that many "value clarifying" activities tend to emphasize conformity rather than the personal development of values. In a perceptive, though perhaps overly harsh, article, John S. Stewart refers to this tendency toward conformity as "coercion to the mean" and offers the following example.

> One of the most frequently used [values clarification] strategies is the "Values Continuum," which involves having students take positions on issues presented on a continuum from one extreme to its opposite. One of the items in this strategy asks, "How do you feel about premarital sex?" The two ends of the continuum are 1) Virginal Virginia (sometimes called Gloves Gladys) and 2) Mattress Millie. Virginal Virginia "wears white gloves on every date" and Mattress Millie "wears a mattress strapped to her back." Now consider the very shy, sensitive, and fearful girl in the class as an extreme example—the girl who's tremendously concerned about her standing with the other girls, or the boys, or the teacher. Suppose

that her position on this issue is clear, even as the result of having applied the principles of Values Clarification, and that she truly believes in either one of the two extreme positions. Would she be likely to affirm publicly such a position in this situation? I would think not. The risks would simply be too great. Assuming that she also does not want to run the risk of being judged somehow for passing (i.e., simply saying "I pass" when asked to comment), one of the legitimate choices in all VC exercises, she might be inclined to express a middle position.

This is what I mean by coercion to the mean, and I see it as a great factor in many of the VC strategies, especially those strategies like the Values Continuum in which the extreme positions are so value-specific, and/or emotionally loaded as to preclude them as legitimate alternatives for public affirmation for many people. Even the middle choice in many cases is equally unacceptable, because of the implications of its wording (e.g., "compulsive moderate"). . . . [Considering] the dynamics of teenage social relationships, the Values Clarification approach can be harmful, or at least can . . . lead to anything but true clarification.[14]

Third, some of the seven requirements that must be fulfilled before a value can result (according to values clarification people) seem themselves open to question. For example, the requirement that students must "publicly affirm" something for it to be a value is misleading. If an individual has never been provided with an opportunity to act on a value—that is, has never been put to the test, so to speak—are we justified in saying that he or she does not possess the value? Furthermore, do we really want to recommend that people must *always* be willing to publicly affirm what they value—even when it is unwise or even dangerous to do so? Isn't that asking for more than most people can produce? And, as noted above, this requirement for public affirmation easily can lead to an over emphasis on conformity, much to the detriment of critical thinking, long a respected and sought-after educational goal.

Likewise, the requirement that an action must be engaged in repeatedly is debatable. What does "repeatedly" mean? Twice? More than twice? Values clarification advocates give us no hints in this regard. It would seem that the number of times a person demonstrates a particular behavior would again depend on the available opportunities for doing so.

Or, consider the emphasis value clarifiers place upon choosing after "thoughtful consideration of the consequences" of alternatives. Unfortunately, they do not explain what such "thoughtful consideration" in-

14 John S. Stewart, "Clarifying Values Clarification: A Critique," *Phi Delta Kappan,* June 1975, p. 685.

volves. What does it mean to "thoughtfully consider" a consequence? How does one do this? What makes one consequence better or worse than another?

Any rational evaluation of consequences requires some set of criteria (characteristics, qualities, and so on) that can be used for comparison. What criteria would the VC people suggest? Are some criteria better than others? Can students be helped to develop such criteria? If so, how? And how does one justify the criteria one uses to evaluate consequences? The values clarification model provides little help to teachers who wish to come to grips with such questions.

Fourth, in its overall purpose, the values clarification model is essentially a personal authentication model. That is, it is directed primarily toward helping students to become more aware of their own personal commitments. But it ignores the fact that personal commitments often conflict. What does a person do when this happens? Suppose that an individual has been taught from childhood to be both loyal and honest. She has internalized and become committed to these values. Suppose that she has observed one of her friends taking money from another student's purse and later is asked by one of her teachers—whom she respects and admires—if she knows anything about the theft? Should she be loyal to her friend and say nothing? Should she be honest and tell the teacher what she has seen? Or should she pursue another alternative? How does she decide? The values clarification model gives little help to individuals dealing with such dilemmas.

The ultimate aim of values clarification is to make students more aware of their own (and others') values. But it does not go beyond this; in effect, it teaches that self-awareness is an end in itself. Such an aim, as noted earlier, teaches that all values are the same, that no value is any better than any other—only "different." Kohlberg offers the following assessment of such a philosophy:

> Values clarification . . . does not attempt to go further than eliciting awareness of values; it is assumed that becoming more self-aware about one's values is an end in itself. Fundamentally, the definition of the end of values education as self-awareness derives from a belief in ethical relativity held by many value-clarifiers. As stated by Peter Engel, "One must contrast value clarification and value inculcation. Value clarification implies the principle that in the consideration of values there is no single correct answer." . . . The teacher is to stress that "our values are different," not that one value is more adequate than others. If this program is systematically followed, students will themselves become relativists, believing there is no "right" moral answer. For instance, a student caught cheating

might argue that he did nothing wrong, since his own hierarchy of values, which may be different from that of the teacher, made it right for him to cheat.[15]

Perhaps the most serious weakness of values clarification, however, and the one for which its advocates can be criticized most severely, is its stated emphasis on the *process* of valuing. This emphasis virtually excludes any stated awareness by the advocates of the need for knowledge about and understanding of the *facts* required to deal intelligently with value issues. Any intelligent discussion of values involves a variety of social, political, and moral issues of considerable complexity. Consider, for example, the value issues imbedded in the following questions.

- Should the death penalty be abolished?
- Should prisons and reformatories emphasize punishment, rehabilitation, or reform?
- Should an individual refuse to obey a law that he or she feels is unjust?
- Should poor people be guaranteed a minimum income whether they work or not?
- Should physicians have the right to end the life of a terminally ill patient upon the patient's request?
- Should members of minority groups be given special consideration in their applications for admission to graduate, professional schools?
- Should women be paid the same as men for similar work?

The above list probably could be extended almost indefinitely. But let us consider a specific example—sex education in the schools. What should children be taught about sex? Before we can even *begin* to discuss this question intelligently, we need to collect a large and diverse amount of information. We need, for example, *facts* about the reproductive process, about fertility, about the most likely times for conception, about various, available methods for preventing conception, and about abortion. We need *facts* about the relationship between feelings and sex, about the effects of emotions on human conduct, about the various motivations for sexual conduct, and about how sexuality can be (and often is) sublimated or expressed in other forms of behavior. We need *facts* about the differing patterns of sexual behavior practiced in different cultures, about sexual customs and taboos, and about how these patterns can affect the total complex of practices that make up a way of life in a society. We need *facts* about the attitudes toward sex of different people and different cultures and about how these attitudes are generated and changed. We need *facts* about how sex has been treated in the theater and in literature and why,

[15] Lawrence Kohlberg, "The Cognitive-Developmental Approach to Moral Education," *Phi Delta Kappan,* June 1975, p. 673.

and about what these forms of expression say about people's sexual attitudes. We also need *facts* about the positions on sex and sex education held by various philosophers, poets, politicians, and even prostitutes and about the arguments they offer to support those positions.

The point being made here is that it is misleading in the extreme to imply that an emphasis on *process* alone can help students come to grips with the issues in value questions. Simply to understand, let alone to try to deal intelligently with such issues, requires the acquisition of a considerable amount of *factual* information. The failure of most value clarifiers [16] to recognize this and to provide for such acquisition as an integral part of their approach is a most serious weakness of the approach.

Finally, it must be noted that values clarification does not help students to appraise critically their own or anyone else's values. Rather, it encourages them to accept uncritically the values of their society. In fact, it teaches that one value is as good as any other. As so many writers have chronicled, however, when a society is in flux (as the United States is today) many conflicting values exist side-by-side; and students acquire a number of values that are in opposition to each other.[17] In the United States, this acquisition of conflicting values cannot be avoided. Yet values clarification does not provide students with any way to deal with the internal (and often external) conflict and uneasiness these opposing values produce. As Hunt and Metcalf once remarked, it doesn't help much to be told that one should always value honesty and kindness when the two conflict.[18] Nor, it might be added, does it help much to be told that these values are equally good (only "different") when one is in a situation where one must choose between them.

The above criticisms are not meant to discourage teachers from using values clarification in the classroom. Rather, they are intended to point up some of the limitations of the approach so that teachers and curriculum developers can begin to think about what else needs to be done to provide for what values clarification ignores. Some suggestions along this line appear in Chapters 5 and 6.

---

1. Read again the criticisms of values clarification on pages 42–47. Do you find them persuasive? Why or why not?

[16] *Values and Teaching* does mention the importance of basing decisions upon facts, but neither it nor other more recent values clarification materials include activities to accomplish it.

[17] See, for example, Gunnar Myrdal, *An American Dilemma* (New York: Harper & Brothers, 1944); Harry S. Broudy, B. Othanel Smith, and Joe R. Burnett, *Democracy and Excellence in American Secondary Education* (Chicago: Rand, McNally & Co., 1964); and Maurice P. Hunt and Lawrence E. Metcalf, *Teaching High School Social Studies* (New York: Harper and Row, 1968).

[18] Hunt and Metcalf, *Teaching High School Social Studies*, p. 124.

2. Values clarification has had a considerable impact among many teachers and has been cited by many writers on curriculum and instruction as an effective approach to values education. How would you account for its popularity? In your opinion, is its popularity justified? Why or why not?

3. On balance, would you say the strengths overshadow the weaknesses of values clarification or vice versa? Why?

EXERCISES

1. Try out some of the activities described in any of the texts listed in the footnote on page 42 or in the works referring to values clarification in the bibliography. What difficulties do you encounter? What suggestions (if any) would you make for changing the activities? Why?

2. Try to devise some value clarifying activities of your own. Think about some aspect of instruction to which values clarification activities might apply. Then try to formulate one or more activities to use with students. What guidelines would you offer to others who want to develop and/or use values clarification activities in the classroom?

3. Try using the same values clarification activities with elementary and secondary school students. Do they work equally well? Why or why not? Are there some values clarification activities that can be used with very young children but not with older children? That should not? Why or why not? What about the reverse?

4. The following incident is taken from *Facing Value Decisions: Rationale-Building for Teachers* by James P. Shaver and William Strong.[19] It suggests one possible outcome of a public interview.

Jeremy and the Public Interview

Problem Which is more important: clarifying values or protecting the privacy of an individual student?

"One more, one more!" the kids were chanting. "C'mon, just one! Please?"

"I don't know," I said. "I don't think so."

The clamor intensified. Any second now I expected my cooperating teacher in the next pod to come bursting in to bring the class back to order.

"Okay, okay," I finally relented in a cowed whisper. "Just hold it down, huh?"

The tenth graders quieted, and I realized that I'd been holding my breath. Just like a runaway stagecoach, I thought to myself.

---

[19] From *Facing Value Decisions: Rationale-Building for Teachers* by James P. Shaver and William Strong, pp. 133–34. © 1976 by Wadsworth Publishing Company, Inc., Belmont, California 94002. Reprinted by permission of the publisher.

Give the horses their head and they'll take you all over the country-side.

"Who'll do the 'public interview' next?" I asked.

"Jeremy's turn!" Liz shouted.

"Yeah, let Jeremy do it!" came another voice.

Jeremy bounded up front and took a round of applause from his audience. I reviewed the rules of the strategy for him: He could either choose the topic or have me suggest one; after we got started he could "pass" on any question he didn't want to answer; and he could terminate the interview whenever he wanted. My job, as teacher, would be to ask questions and make clarifying responses.

"I want to be interviewed about *drugs*," Jeremy said in a cool, worldly way. "You know—like narcotics and that."

The class began hooting and giggling. "Okay," I nodded. "Would you like to tell us what you think about drugs?"

"Yeah. Like there's a lot of it going down at this school." He grinned at a buddy.

"You think it's a problem, then?"

"Yeah, you could say that. I mean, you start fooling around with some of that junk and it scrambles the circuitry upstairs."

"Well, how many kids do you think are using drugs regularly as opposed to experimentally?"

"Some of both." Jeremy winked. "But mostly just messing around, I guess. Like, you know, grass and pills—stuff like that."

"What's behind this experimentation?"

Jeremy hesitated and his mood semed to grow a shade quieter. "I don't know," he said slowly. "Something to do, I guess—just being in with the guys. Or maybe just to see what it's like. Or to get back at your old man and old lady. There could be a hundred different reasons."

"That makes sense."

"I mean, maybe you're at this party and somebody starts a joint moving around. It's pretty hard to pass it up when everybody's watching."

"So it starts innocently enough," I said. "But—

"But then they *expect* you to smoke after that," Jeremy said, "whether you want to or not."

My throat was dry and tense. "That could be a pretty tough problem," I said.

"Yeah."

"I'm not entirely sure of your attitude toward drugs," I said. "On the one hand, you seem to take a kind of cavalier attitude. But you also seem to regard the drug scene as a really serious problem—"

"Well, some of that stuff can really screw up your head," Jeremy interrupted. "I mean, so you can't think straight, you know?" The classroom was utterly quiet.

"We're running short of time," I said. "Maybe we'd better wind this up."

"I remember this one time that me and Andy Elliott and some other guys—Cleaver and Butch—"

"Jeremy, I'd like to conclude this interview."

"Cleaver was really flipped out. I mean, like it was *really* a bad trip. Anyhow, the awful part was—"

Dave Cleaver lunged out of his desk and through the open classroom door. The sound of his running echoed down the hall.

Shaver and Strong do not mean to imply that all values clarification exercises will end up like the fictional one above. They present this episode as an admittedly extreme example to raise some questions about the overall approach, among which are these two:

a. Is there any point in the story where you would have directed the discussion in a different way?

b. If you were the teacher conducting the class, what would you do now about Dave Cleaver?

Think also about these questions:

c. Would you have asked any additional or different questions of Jeremy? If so, what would you have asked?

d. Would you have responded differently at any point? If so, what would you have said? And why?

e. Are there any topics about which you would not hold a public interview even if students wanted one? If so, what are they? Would the age of the children being interviewed affect your answer in any way? If so, how? And why?

How realistic is this incident?

chapter four

MORAL REASONING

Recently, a number of educators have been arguing for the development of "moral" reasoning—that is, reasoning about moral issues—in elementary and secondary school classrooms, particularly in the social studies. The essence of this approach lies in engaging students in the discussion of "moral dilemmas" and then exposing them to different justifications given by other students or the teacher for various resolutions of those dilemmas.

A moral dilemma is a situation in which an individual is faced with a choice of two or more courses of action, both (or all) of which are possible and feasible under the circumstances. None of the courses of action, however, can be followed without producing some sort of physical or mental conflict or stress. The following is an example of a moral dilemma. A police officer is faced with choosing between allowing a soapbox speaker to continue before an increasingly angry crowd or ordering the speaker to stop. The first choice respects the speaker's constitutional right to speak out in public, but also may endanger his personal safety. The second alternative protects the speaker from possible violence but also may infringe on his constitutional rights. Moral dilemmas can be found among a variety of sources including newspaper articles, advertisements, comic strips, cartoons, plays, and films.

The leading contemporary advocate of the development of moral reasoning is Professor Lawrence Kohlberg of Harvard University. Much of his work has its roots in the thinking of John Dewey but also and especially in the stage theory of Jean Piaget. Before we describe and discuss Kohlberg's theory, let us look at some of Piaget's conclusions.

51

PIAGET'S STAGE THEORY

Piaget's original training was in the natural sciences. Though his main interest at first was in biology (he published more than twenty scientific papers before he was twenty-one) he also became interested early in his career in the intellectual development of children. Over the last fifty years he has concentrated on systematically investigating and describing such development.

Piaget views cognitive development as a process that takes place naturally as children grow, mature, and interact with their environment. He states that there are certain periods of cognitive development that all children go through, though not all necessarily reach the highest period— that of formal operations (see Table 1). Though most children tend to move through these periods at about the ages indicated, some move sooner, others move later.

Piaget views these periods as cumulative and sequential. A child's development proceeds through the stages as they are listed in Table 1 and in that order. People do not skip stages. Furthermore, each period is viewed as a prerequisite or foundation for what follows. Each period, in effect, represents a time of growth in a child's life when he or she becomes able to think *differently* than was possible during an earlier period. Also, a person may be in more than one period—at more than one stage of development—at the same time. Thus a child may vary in the type of thinking of which he or she is capable from time to time or when faced with different sorts of tasks.

Piaget also has studied the moral development of children, and his conclusions in this regard are consistent with his conclusions about intellectual development in general. He sees moral development as proceeding through a sequence of three stages: (1) a blind-obedience stage, involving "objective moral judgments" in which a child's idea of what is right or wrong is based simply on what his parents permit or forbid him to do; (2) an interpretation-of-rules stage during which the child learns that the spirit rather than the letter of a rule is more important (shifting from "moral realism" to "moral relativism") and makes "subjective" value judgments; and (3) an interpretation-of-the-act stage, during which the child develops a sense of personal and ethical responsibility for his or her behavior.

Piaget has not been interested in the moral *behavior* of children so much as he has in the ways in which they think about moral *issues*. The first major change in such thinking, he has observed, occurs at about age seven. Prior to that, children supposedly judge deviant acts solely in terms

TABLE 1   Piaget's periods of cognitive development

Sensori-Motor Period (0–2 Years)

Stage 1 (0–1 months):	Reflex actions only.
Stage 2 (1–4 months):	Hand-mouth coordination.
Stage 3 (4–8 months):	Hand-eye coordination.
Stage 4 (8–12 months):	Means-ends behavior begins.
	Absent objects take on permanence (child will search for articles taken out of sight).
Stage 5 (12–18 months):	Tries out different means (experiments) to get what he wants.
Stage 6 (18–24 months):	External objects are represented in the mind; symbols are used.
	Thinks out different means to get what he wants.

Preoperational Period (2–7 Years)

Problems are solved through thinking about them.
Rapid language (2–4 years) and conceptual development takes place.
Thought and language are egocentric (they reflect the child's point of view, not the views of others).
Orientation is perceptual (judgments are made in terms of how things look to the child).
Imagined or apparent and real events are confused ("magical" thinking).
Attention tends to center on one thing at a time.

Concrete Operational Period (7–11 Years)

Reversibility is attained (understands, e.g., that the volume of liquid is the same even if the shape of the container is changed).
Logical operations develop and are applied to concrete problems.
Complex verbal problems cannot be solved yet.

Formal Operations Period (11–15 Years)

All types of logical problems, including deductive hypothesis testing, and complex verbal and hypothetical problems can be solved.
Analysis of the validity of ways of reasoning becomes possible.
Formal thought is still egocentric in the sense that there is difficulty in squaring ideals with reality.

---

of the *damage* they produce. Between seven and eleven, children enter the stage of subjective morality and judge a transgression in terms of *intent*. Piaget observed this shift in thinking by presenting young children with pairs of stories in which the characters differ both in terms of their intentions and the amount of damage that they do, as in the following.

> 1. John was in his room when his mother called him to dinner. John goes down and opens the door to the dining room. But behind the door was a chair, and on the chair was a tray with fifteen cups on it. John did not

know the cups were behind the door. He opens the door, the door hits the tray, bang go the fifteen cups, and they all get broken.

2. One day when Henry's mother was out, Henry tried to get some cookies out of the cupboard. He climbed up on chair; but the cookie jar was still too high, and he couldn't reach it. But while he was trying to get the cookie jar, he knocked over a cup. The cup fell down and broke.

Children are asked to judge which of the two characters (in this case, John or Henry) is the naughtier. In general, younger children say that John is naughtier, because he broke fifteen cups. Older children (over seven) find Henry naughtier, because he engaged in an act that his mother had forbidden.

At about the age of eleven, the child makes a third shift when he enters the period of formal operations and develops the ability to identify and use abstract principles. It is during this period that the ability to analyze the valdity of different ways of reasoning develops.

---

1. Refer to Table 1. What do you think is the lowest level of development at which a student still could be able to engage in each of the following operations? Why?

a. Identifying things that he or she considers important.

b. Making inferences about the values of other people based on observation of their actions in a specific situation.

c. Comparing and contrasting the values of different people after observing their actions in a number of situations.

d. Identifying the positions of different people involved in a controversial issue.

e. Telling another person what he or she (the speaker) likes.

2. What kinds of activities do you think would *not* work with children at the preoperational level? The concrete operational? Why?

3. In what kinds of value issues might students at the concrete operational level be interested? The formal operational level? Why? Are there some kinds of issues that students at the formal operational level would be able to discuss but those at the concrete operational would *not*? Might this depend on how the issue was presented to the students?

4. All people who are not intellectually retarded are expected to reach Piaget's level of concrete operations, though not necessarily by age 7. Some researchers [1] have suggested, however, that as many as 40 percent of all adults in the United States may not attain the level of formal operations. If this is true, what implications might it have for values education in the schools?

KOHLBERG'S STAGE THEORY

Building on Piaget's work, especially his research in moral development, Kohlberg has developed a similar but more elaborate theory. Kohl-

---

[1] Lawrence Kohlberg and Carol Gilligan, "The Adolescent as a Philosopher: The Discovery of the Self in a Postconventional World," *Daedalus*, Vol. 100, 1971, p. 1065.

berg specifically has incorporated several Piagetian concepts into his own work—particularly the ideas of stage sequence and of conflict, dissonance, and imbalance—as necessary before further intellectual development results.

James Rest has identified three fundamental ideas lying at the heart of Kohlberg's theory. These he labeled "structural organization," "developmental sequence," and "interactionism." [2] *Structural organization* refers to the fact that developmental psychologists such as Kohlberg consider the development of a person's cognitive structure of crucial importance in that person's overall growth and development. Cognitive structure is the way a person analyzes and interprets data and makes decisions about personal and social problems. *Developmental sequence* refers to the view of Kohlberg and others that the development of a person's cognitive structure occurs in terms of stages. According to this view the developmentally earlier and less complex "lower" stages are prerequisites to the "higher" stages. A major purpose of education for a developmentalist is to foster individual movement through these stages

Using hypothetical, ethical dilemmas (e.g., "Should a doctor 'mercy kill' a fatally ill patient who is requesting death because of pain?"), Kohlberg interviewed children and adults in the United States, Turkey, Taiwan, Mexico, and Malaysia. He then classified their responses into six groups in terms of the *types of reasons* they gave. In all of the cultures he studied, he identified three levels of moral development—the preconventional, the conventional, and the post conventional. Each of these levels has two stages in it, for a total of six stages of moral reasoning (see Table 2).

Preconventional children, though often "well-behaved" in a stereotypical sense and responsive to cultural labels of what is good or bad, act either because of the physical consequences involved (punishment, reward, exchange of favors) or because of the physical powers of authority figures (parents, teachers, and so on).

Children at the conventional level tend toward conformity. Living up to the expectations and maintaining the rules or laws of one's family, group, or nation is considered good in its own right. Concern is shown not only for conforming to but also for supporting and justifying the social order. According to Kohlberg, most adult Americans are at this level.

At the third level, the postconventional, individuals tend to think in terms of autonomous moral principles rooted in the concept of justice that they conceive as universally applicable. Such principles are considered distinct from the authority of the individuals or groups who hold them as well as from a person's affiliation with those individuals or groups.

---

[2] James Rest, "Developmental Psychology as a Guide to Value Education: A Review of 'Kohlbergian' Programs," *Review of Educational Research*, Spring 1974, pp. 241–259.

TABLE 2   Kohlberg's stages of moral development

Preconventional Level

Stage 1:   Punishment and obedience orientation. The physical consequences of an act determine whether it is good or bad, regardless of the meaning or value of these consequences to an individual. Avoidance of punishment and unquestioning obedience to superiors are valued in their own right.

Stage 2:   Instrumental relativist orientation. What satisfies one's own and occasionally others' needs is good. "You scratch my back and I'll scratch yours" is a prevailing attitude of individuals at this stage.

Conventional Level

Stage 3:   Interpersonal concordance or "good boy–nice girl" orientation. What pleases or helps others and is approved by them is good. There is much conformity to stereotypical notions of what is "natural" or "nice" or majority behavior. Behavior is frequently judged by intention ("She means well").

Stage 4:   "Law and order" orientation. Maintaining the social order, showing respect for authority, and doing one's duty is good. One earns respect by obeying fixed rules, laws, and authority.

Postconventional Level

Stage 5:   Social contract legalistic orientation. Values agreed upon by the society, including individual rights and rules for consensus, determine what is right. There is an emphasis upon rules of *procedure* for reaching consensus. The emphasis is on "the legal point of view," but with stress on the possibility of *changing* law in terms of rational considerations or social usefulness, rather than freezing it in terms of "law and order" as at Stage 4. Aside from what is constitutionally and democratically agreed upon, what is right or wrong is a matter of personal values.

Stage 6:   Universal ethical-principle orientation. What is right is a matter of conscience in accord with self-chosen principles viewed as logical, consistent, and universal. These principles are abstract and ethical (e.g., the Golden Rule) as opposed to the concrete moral rules (e.g., the Ten Commandments) of Stage 4. These universal principles in essence are the principles of justice, of the reciprocity and equality of human rights, and of the respect for the dignity of human beings as individual persons.

Adapted from L. Kohlberg, "Moral Education in Schools," *School Review,* Spring 1966, p. 7. Copyright 1966, University of Chicago. By permission of University of Chicago Press.

The single soldier who refused orders to participate in the massacre at the Vietnamese village of My Lai in 1968 was identified as being at this level.

The stage of moral reasoning that a particular child has achieved is determined by having judges evaluate the child's responses to a hypothetical "moral dilemma"—a story in which an individual is faced with choosing from among conflicting alternatives. These stories are philosophical in nature and involve questions of responsibility, motive, or intention. Here is an example:

In Europe, a woman was near death from cancer. One drug might save her, a form of radium that a druggist in the same town had recently discovered. The druggist was charging $2,000, ten times what the drug cost him to make. The sick woman's husband, Heinz, went to everyone he knew to borrow the money, but he could only get together about half of what it cost. He told the druggist that his wife was dying and asked him to sell it cheaper or let him pay later. But the druggist said, "no." The husband got desperate and broke into the man's store to steal the drug for his wife. Should the husband have done that? Why? [3]

To gain a further idea of the type of moral judgment that students make in response to such stories, consider some examples of responses made to the dilemma faced by Heinz in the above story. Notice that the stages of moral reasoning are not differentiated by the nature of the decision itself, but rather on the basis of the *reasons* given for the decision.

Pro	*Stage 6*	*Con*
If you don't steal the drug and let your wife die, you'd always condemn yourself for it afterward. You wouldn't be blamed and you would have lived up to the outside rule of the law but you wouldn't have lived up to your own standards of conscience.	Concern about self-condemnation for violating one's own principles. (Differentiates between community respect and self-respect. Differentiates between self-respect for general achieving rationality and self-respect for maintaining moral principles.)	If you stole the drug, you wouldn't be blamed by other people but you'd condemn yourself because you wouldn't have lived up to your own conscience and standards of honesty.

Pro	*Stage 5*	*Con*
You'd lose other people's respect, not gain it, if you don't steal. If you let your wife die, it would be out of fear, not out of reasoning it out. So you'd just lose self-respect and probably the respect of others too.	Concern about maintaining respect of equals and of the community (assuming their respect is based on reason rather than emotions). Concern about own self-respect, i.e., to avoid judging self as irrational, inconsistent, non-purposive.	You would lose your standing and respect in the community and violate the law. You'd lose respect for yourself if you're carried away by emotion and forget the long-range point of view.

[3] Lawrence Kohlberg, "Stage and Sequence: The Cognitive-Developmental Approach to Socialization," in D. Goslin (ed.), *Handbook of Socialization Theory and Research* (Chicago: Rand McNally, 1969).

Pro	*Stage 4*	*Con*
If you have any sense of honor, you won't let your wife die because you're afraid to do the only thing that will save her. You'll always feel guilty that you caused her death if you don't do your duty to her.	Action motivated by anticipation of dishonor, i.e., institutionalized blame for failure of duty, and by guilt over concrete harm done to others. (Differentiates formal dishonor from informal disapproval. Differentiates guilt for bad consequences from disapproval.)	You're desperate and you may not know you're doing wrong when you steal the drug. But you'll know you did wrong after you're punished and sent to jail. You'll always feel guilty for your dishonesty and lawbreaking.

Pro	*Stage 3*	*Con*
No one will think you're bad if you steal the drug but your family will think you're an inhuman husband if you don't. If you let your wife die, you'll never be able to look anybody in the face again.	Action motivated by anticipation of disapproval of others, actual or imagined-hypothetical (e.g., guilt). (Differentiation of disapproval from punishment, fear, and pain.)	It isn't just the druggist who will think you're a criminal, everyone else will too. After you steal it, you'll feel bad thinking how you've brought dishonor on your family and yourself; you won't be able to face anyone again.

Pro	*Stage 2*	*Con*
If you do happen to get caught you could give the drug back and you wouldn't get much of a sentence. It wouldn't bother you much to serve a little jail term, if you have your wife when you get out.	Action motivated by desire for reward or benefit. Possible guilt reactions are ignored and punishment viewed in a pragmatic manner. (Differentiates own fear, pleasure, or pain from punishment-consequences.)	He may not get much of a jail term if he steals the drug, but his wife will probably die before he gets out so it won't do him much good. If his wife dies, he shouldn't blame himself, it wasn't his fault she has cancer.

Pro	*Stage 1*	*Con*
If you let your wife die, you will get in trouble. You'll be blamed for not spending the money to save her and there'll be an investigation of you and the druggist for your wife's death.	Action is motivated by avoidance of punishment, and "conscience" is irrational fear of punishment.	You shouldn't steal the drug because you'll be caught and sent to jail if you do. If you do get away, your conscience would bother you thinking how the police would catch up with you at any minute.

Like Piaget, Kohlberg argues that progression through these stages is sequential and invariant but also that not all people reach the highest stages. (He estimates that less than 20 percent of adult Americans reason at the postconventional level.) [4] Furthermore, he believes that the six stages are universal, hold true in all cultures, and that each stage represents a level of reasoning higher than the one immediately preceding it. He came to this conclusion by observing that no subjects found to be at Stages 1 through 4 had gone through Stages 5 or 6; however, those individuals at Stages 5 or 6 all had gone through Stages 1 through 4. Though individuals do not skip stages, they may move through them quickly or slowly and may be found half in and half out of a particular stage at any given time. As individuals progress through the stages, they become increasingly able to take in and synthesize more and different information than they could at earlier stages. They become better able to organize this information into an integrated and systematized framework. Moral thought, then, is viewed as operating in the same manner as any other kind of thought. Kohlberg also has argued that higher-stage reasoning is morally better than lower-stage reasoning. [5]

Interactionism refers to the process by which a person's cognitive structure is developed. As a child develops and notices certain regularities in his environment, she develops a pattern of behavior (a cognitive structure) to deal with these regularities—a way of thinking about the world. As the child grows and matures, however, she undergoes experiences for which her previously developed cognitive structure is inadequate. She thus seeks to revamp her way of thinking in order to make sense of the new experience. When she finds a new way of thinking that enables her to understand the experience, her cognitive structure—her way of thinking about the world—is changed accordingly. An essential ingredient for intellectual growth—for the cognitive development of the child—therefore, is the opportunity to engage in a number of new and different experiences that will cause her to try to reorder her way of thinking and to seek out more adequate ways to organize and interpret data.

What does this mean for teachers? What implications does Kohlberg's theory have for values education? The most significant implication, perhaps, lies in Kohlberg's argument that progression through the stages is a *natural* development, one that teachers can further by presenting students with such moral dilemmas as the one involving Heinz and his wife and by then discussing what the character(s) involved should do. The teacher must ensure, however, that students are exposed to the arguments

4 Lawrence Kohlberg, "The Concepts of Developmental Psychology as the Central Guide to Education: Examples from Cognitive, Moral, and Psychological Education," in *The Proceedings of the Conference on Psychology and the Process of Schooling in the Next Decade: Alternative Conceptions* (Minneapolis: University of Minnesota Audio-Visual Extension, 1971).
5 Lawrence Kohlberg, "The Cognitive-Developmental Approach to Moral Education," *Phi Delta Kappan,* June 1975, pp. 672–673.

of individuals who are reasoning *one* stage *above* their own level. Kohlberg suggests that children and adolescents *prefer* the highest level of moral reasoning that they can understand. They are able to comprehend all stages lower than their own, as well as one stage higher than their own and even, on occasion, two stages higher than their own.[6] They tend to reject the arguments of individuals reasoning at lower stages, finding them simplistic and in some cases naive. But they usually cannot understand the arguments of those who are reasoning more than one stage above their own. Students with extensive peer-group participation (i.e., discussion of moral dilemmas) were found to advance more quickly than students without such participation.[7]

---

1. Many characters in films and literature can be identified as being at different levels of moral development. Mary Poppins, for example, has been viewed as a perfect Stage 3, the Japanese Colonel Saito in the movie *Bridge on the River Kwai* as being at Stage 4, and Joan of Arc as a Stage 6 type. What examples would you suggest of individuals from literature who might be considered at different levels and stages of moral thinking? What about the statements made by public figures in the daily press and other media? What stages of moral reasoning do their statements suggest?

2. Here is an example of the type of ethical question that Kohlberg has asked children: "Should a doctor 'mercy-kill' a fatally ill woman requesting death because of her pain?" Below are several examples of responses that individuals of different ages have given to this question. At which of Kohlberg's stages would you judge each of these respondents to be?

Answer Given	Reason Offered in Support of Answer
1. Yes,	because she would be such a burden to her family and to herself too.
2. No,	because it's against the law.
3. No,	because only God has the right to take a life. He'd almost be destroying a part of God if he helped her to die.
4. No,	because the value of life takes precedence over every other value there is. A person's life has value in and of itself, whether the person values it or not. No one—a doctor, a lawyer, or anyone—should deal trivially with a person's life.
5. Yes,	because she is suffering and has a lot of pain.
6. No,	because they might not be able to afford how much it would cost.
7. Yes,	because the doctor would lose his self-respect as a man if he didn't help her.
8. Yes,	because she has asked to die, and her family is probably suffering a lot.
9. Yes,	because it's her own choice. More and more doctors and nurses are beginning to believe that it is a hardship on everyone—the person, the family—when someone is kept alive who is terminally ill and doesn't want to live anymore. And if she would have to be kept alive by an artificial limb or kidney or some other means, it's more like being a vegetable than a

[6] Kohlberg, "Moral Education in the Schools," p. 17.
[7] Ibid.

human being. There are certain inherent rights that go with being a human being—you, me, everyone. In that respect we're all equal.

DISCUSSING MORAL DILEMMAS IN THE CLASSROOM

How does a teacher go about engaging students in a discussion of a moral dilemma? What procedures and/or techniques does he or she employ? Galbraith and Jones [8] and Beyer [9] have developed a model teaching strategy for conducting moral discussions that includes three parts: a list of general instructions for presenting the original dilemma, a series of alternative dilemmas to use in case the original dilemma fails to promote controversy, and a list of probe questions. Galbraith and Jones argue that "although alternative dilemmas involve the same story, the same characters, and the same moral issues, they change the situation described in the original problem in an effort to promote disagreement about what the main character should do." [10] Let us look at an example of such alternative dilemmas and probe questions, together with the original dilemma they were first designed to accompany, followed by a description and illustration of how to use them in the classroom.

Helga's Dilemma

Helga and Rachel had grown up together. They were best friends despite the fact that Helga's family was Christian and Rachel's was Jewish. For many years, this religious difference didn't seem to matter much in Germany, but after Hitler seized power the situation changed. Hitler required Jews to wear armbands with the Star of David on them. He began to encourage his followers to destroy the property of Jewish people and to beat them on the street. Finally, he began to arrest Jews and deport them. Rumors went around the city that many Jews were being killed. Hiding Jews for whom the Gestapo (Hitler's secret police) was looking was a serious crime and violated a law of the German government.

One night Helga heard a knock at the door. When she opened it, she found Rachel on the step huddled in a dark coat. Quickly Rachel stepped inside. She had been to a meeting, she said, and when she returned home she had found Gestapo members all around

8 Ronald E. Galbraith and Thomas M. Jones, "Teaching Strategies for Moral Dilemmas: An Application of Kohlberg's Theory of Moral Development to the Social Studies Classroom," *Social Education,* January 1975, pp. 16–22. Excerpts reprinted by permission of the publisher and authors.
9 Barry K. Beyer, "Conducting Moral Discussions in the Classroom" *Social Education,* April 1976, pp. 194–202. Excerpts reprinted by permission of the publisher and author.
10 Galbraith and Jones, "Teaching Strategies," p. 19.

her house. Her parents and brothers had already been taken away. Knowing her fate if the Gestapo caught her, Rachel ran to her old friend's house.

Now what should Helga do? If she turned Rachel away, the Gestapo would eventually find her. Helga knew that most of the Jews who were sent away had been killed, and she didn't want her best friend to share that fate. But hiding the Jews broke the law. Helga would risk her own security and that of her family if she tried to hide Rachel. But she had a tiny room behind the chimney on the third floor where Rachel might be safe.

Question: Should Helga hide Rachel?

Alternative Dilemmas

If the class agrees that Helga *should* hide Rachel, one of the following alternative dilemmas can be used to provoke disagreement.

A. Suppose Helga had only met Rachel once and did not know her well. What should she do in that case?

B. Suppose Helga's father and mother heard what was happening at the door and told her not to let Rachel in the house. In that case what should she do?

If the class agrees that Helga *should not* hide Rachel, one of the following alternative dilemmas can be used to provoke disagreement.

A. Suppose that several of Helga's friends were also hiding Jews from the Gestapo. What should Helga do in that case?

B. Suppose Helga heard the Gestapo coming and knew that Rachel would be shot on sight within a few minutes if she did not hide her. What should she do in that case?

Probe Questions

1. What is the most important thing that one friend owes to another? Why?

2. Should a person ever risk the welfare of relatives for the welfare of friends? Why?

3. Should a person ever risk his or her own life for someone else? Why?

4. Is a person ever justified to hide someone who is fleeing from the authorities?

5. From Rachel's point of view, what should Helga do?

6. From the point of view of Helga's father, what should Helga do? [11]

Beyer [12] suggests five distinct activities in which teachers might en-

11 Galbraith and Jones, "Teaching Strategies," pp. 18–19.
12 Beyer, "Conducting Moral Discussions," pp. 196–197.

gage students as a part of discussing such dilemmas as the one above (see Figure 4-1). They include the following.

1. Presenting the dilemma (introducing, in written, oral, audio, or visual form, a particular dilemma situation for the class to consider). He suggests that it is sometimes useful first to prepare students for the kind of situation presented in the dilemma by

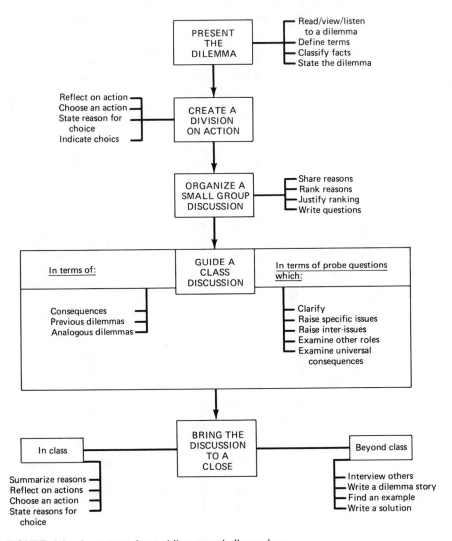

FIGURE 4-1 A strategy for guiding moral discussions.

Taken from Beyer, "Conducting Moral Discussions," p. 199.

mentioning or asking questions about related, present-day examples of such situations.

2. Recommending tentative courses of action to resolve the dilemma and justifying these recommendations (encouraging students to take a tentative position about what particular action he or she thinks the central figure in the dilemma should take).

3. Discussing the reasoning behind their recommendations in small groups. Beyer recommends that there should be about a 75–25 split about what should be done before this discussion should commence. He argues that the most productive moral discussions occur when small group interactions are followed by a discussion involving the entire class. Furthermore, the teacher should move from group to group, helping students to focus on the moral issues involved in the dilemma. Two grouping arrangements are possible. "Where the class division on action is uneven, groups of from four to six students can be created in which all members of each group hold the same position. The students in a group can list all the reasons they have for their position, choose the best of these reasons, and then state why this reason is the best one. With a fairly even class division about action, the teacher can organize groups in which an equal number of students represent opposing positions. The group members can discuss their positions and reasons in order to make a list of the two best reasons for each position represented. Students should feel free to switch from one group to another if, in the midst of a group discussion, they decide to change their position on action. When these group tasks have been completed, students can then convene as an entire class to continue their discussion." [13]

4. Examining as a class their reasoning and the reasoning others use as they justify recommended solutions to the dilemma. The purpose here is to give students an opportunity to report on the reasoning behind their position and to hear the reasoning behind the positions of others, to challenge others' reasoning, and to have their own reasoning challenged. "The process of stating, challenging, being challenged, defending, explaining, criticizing, and comparing highlights the existence of a gap between one's own stage of reasoning and the reasoning at the next higher stage. In time, students become conscious of this gap and move to close it." [14] An important part of the general class discussion is the teacher's use of probe questions such as those on pages 62 and 67. They help students examine issues they had ignored or not thought about previously.

5. Reflecting on their own and others' reasoning. The chief task here is to bring the discussion to a close. Students can be asked to summarize all of the reasons they have heard and to choose the one they consider most persuasive. Beyer states that public declaration

[13] Ibid., p. 197.
[14] Ibid.

of their choice is "neither necessary nor desirable, for doing so might imply that there is a correct answer, an assumption antithetical to this entire strategy." [15]

Here is an example of a dilemma designed for use by junior high school students, followed by a teaching plan Beyer developed to illustrate how each of the five basic activities can be used to guide a moral discussion.

Sharon and Jill were best friends. One day they went shopping together. Jill tried on a sweater and then, to Sharon's surprise, walked out of the store wearing the sweater under her coat. A moment later, the store's security officer stopped Sharon and demanded that she tell him the name of the girl who had walked out. He told the storeowner that he had seen the two girls together, and that he was sure that the one who left had been shoplifting. The storeowner told Sharon that she could really get in trouble if she didn't give her friend's name.[16]

Teaching Plan for Sharon's Dilemma [17]

Part I—Presenting the Dilemma

Distribute the handout which describes Sharons dilemma. Make sure that the students understand any difficult terms or phrases in the dilemma. Have the students clarify the facts of the situation. Have a volunteer state and explain the nature of the moral dilemma Sharon faces.

Part II—Dividing on Action

Ask the students to think for a moment about what they think Sharon should do. They should then write their recommendation and reason for their recommendation on a sheet of paper. Determine by a show of hands or in some other way how many students think Sharon should or should not tell her friend's name to the security officer. Have a volunteer representing each position explain the reasons for their positions.

If the class fails to divide satisfactorily, use the following alternatives as appropriate:

If the members of the class agree that Sharon *should* tell:

1. Suppose Sharon knows that Jill is on parole and will be sent back to a reformatory if she is caught stealing. What should she do in that case?
2. Suppose that Jill has done Sharon many favors and that Sharon knows

15 Ibid., p. 198.
16 Ibid., p. 194.
17 Ibid., pp. 201–202.

that she will lose many of her friends if she tells on Jill. What should she do in that case?

If the members of the class agree that Sharon *should not* tell:

1. Suppose that on a previous occasion, Jill had told their teacher that Sharon had cheated on an examination. What should Sharon do in that case?
2. Suppose that instead of being a friend, Jill was only an acquaintance whom Sharon knew casually. What should Sharon do in that case?

If the alternative dilemmas fail to provoke a division, have students role play different sides of the dilemma or have them revise the dilemma and then take positions. Then have volunteers representing each position explain the reasons for their positions.

Part III—Small Group Discussions

When the class divides with no less than one-quarter of the students on each side of the issue, organize a small group discussion in which students can share their reasons, choose those reasons they think are best for the position recommended, and decide why these reasons are their "best" reasons.

Part IV—Class Discussion

Reconvene the class in a large group. Have students from each small group report the group decisions or list their decisions on the board. Encourage students to discuss the merits of the reasons given by each group. Use some of the following probe questions where appropriate to focus the discussion:

1. What is a "best friend?"
2. Does Sharon have an obligation to Jill? the store owner? the law? herself? Why or why not?
3. Which set of obligations, to Jill, to the store owner, or to the law, are most important? Why?
4. From the point of view of Jill (of the store owner, of Sharon's parents) should Sharon tell? Why or why not?
5. Is it ever right to tell on a friend? Why or why not?

Part V—Closing the Discussion

Have the students who feel that Sharon should tell summarize all the reasons given by those who argued that Sharon should not tell. Have the students who said Sharon should not tell summarize the reasons given by those who argued Sharon should tell. Then have the students think about what they have heard, choose again what they think Sharon should do, and write their choice and a reason for their choice on a piece of paper. Do *not* collect the papers.

1. What do you think is the central issue involved in Helga's dilemma? In Sharon's?

2. What other alternatives to Helga's dilemma can you suggest? To Sharon's?

3. What other probe questions would you ask about each of these dilemmas? Why?

4. Beyer has suggested five kinds of probe questions that might be used during a general class discussion of a dilemma. He describes them as follows:

> A clarifying probe calls on students to define terms they have used or to explain a comment which does not convey reasoning. For example, if a student says "I think that stealing is immoral," the teacher might respond with a clarifying probe, "What do you mean by immoral?" An issue-specific probe encourages a student to examine their thoughts about one of the nine major issues which Kohlberg argues provide a focus for moral reasoning. In discussing Sharon's dilemma an example of such a probe question might be "What obligations do you owe to a friend?" This question gets at the specific issue of affectional relations. An inter-issue probe encourages students to think about what to do when a conflict occurs between two separate issues: "Which is more important, loyalty to a friend or the obligation to obey the law? Why?" A role-switch probe puts the students in the position of someone else involved in the dilemma in order to get them to see another side of the problem. Such a question might be "From the point of view of Jill's parents, should Sharon tell?" Finally, a universal consequence probe asks students to consider what might happen if such a position or such reasoning were applied to everyone. For example, "Is it ever right to tell on a friend?" [18]

Can you think of any other types of such questions that might be asked? Are there any sorts of questions that students should *not* be asked? Why? Which of the five types that Beyer lists (if any) do you think is the most important to ask of students? The least important? Why?

5. Can you see any disadvantages in having students discuss moral dilemmas? What might they be?

MORAL DISCUSSIONS AT THE ELEMENTARY LEVEL

Galbraith and Jones recommend using the same basic strategy with elementary school students, only with some slight modifications. For example, when introducing the dilemma, they recommend asking students some warm-up questions to allow them to begin early to identify with the circumstances of the dilemma. They also suggest the following:

1. Using dilemmas in films, filmstrips, and audio-tapes for more variety.
2. Discussing the dilemma in general before asking the class to indicate a tentative position.

[18] Ibid., p. 198.

3. Dividing the class into small groups later, rather than earlier in the discussion as with secondary level students.

4. Expanding on the story—by presenting the class with an "additional chapter" in the story, so to speak (rather than presenting a series of alternative dilemmas as with secondary students).

Here is an example of a dilemma available on film and the corresponding teaching plan they suggest for use at the elementary level.[19]

"Who Needs Rules?"

The film presents two situations in which children are torn between obeying or breaking a rule. In the first episode, Steve and Connie find a stray puppy in the park. Steve wants to keep it, but Connie reminds him of their apartment building's rule prohibiting pets. Steve is concerned about the puppy's health, however, and decides to take the dog home to feed it. Connie also feels attached to the unfortunate pup, but reminds Steve of the rule and worries that the family will be evicted if a pet is discovered. Steve's desire to give the puppy a good home conflicts with Connie's practical observations. They are left to make their difficult decision as the projector is stopped. The viewers then consider what they would do in this situation.[20]

Teaching Plan: "Who Needs Rules?"

A. Warm-Up Questions

1. How many of you have ever had a puppy?
2. How many of you have ever found a puppy in a park, on a playground or in your neighborhood?
3. Does anybody here live in an apartment building? Do you know whether apartment buildings have rules concerning animals or pets? What are some of the rules?
4. Have you ever heard of an apartment building that has a rule saying you cannot have pets in the building?
5. Who knows what an animal shelter is? What happens when puppies are taken to an animal shelter?

B. Presentation

Show the first segment of the film to the class. Begin the film at the place where it shows a sign in the park and Connie and Steve

19 Ronald E. Galbraith and Thomas M. Jones, *Moral Reasoning: A Teaching Handbook for Adapting Kohlberg to the Classroom* (Minneapolis: Greenhaven Press, Inc., 1967), pp. 172–80. Reprinted by permission of Greenhaven Press, Inc., 1611 Polk St. N.E., Minneapolis, Minnesota 55413.
20 From "Who Needs Rules?" Encyclopaedia Britannica Educational Corporation (Chicago, 1972).

playing with a Frisbee, search for the Frisbee in the shrubbery, and finding a puppy. Run the film through the place where Steve says, "Look, I can't take care of him all by myself. But if you help, we can do it, at least for the summer. Come on, Connie, do we try it or not?" At this point, a narrator asks several questions. These questions can be used as part of the initiating questions for the discussion.

C. Initiating Questions

Clarify the circumstances, terms, and characters in the story. The following questions should help to determine how individual students respond to the dilemma story and whether the class disagrees over the action position for the central characters in the story.

1. What should Steve and Connie do?
2. Why does the apartment have a rule against pets?
3. Do Steve and Connie have a right to break that rule?
4. Should Steve and Connie tell anyone else about their puppy in the storeroom?
5. What is the best thing for Steve and Connie to do so that they can help the puppy?

Note: Be sure to give as many students as possible a chance to respond to the initiating questions so that you can determine if they have different viewpoints on the story. Frequently ask students to respond to another student comment. For example: "David, do you also agree with Lisa's comment, or do you have some other idea to add?" or "Susan, a lot of people here think it's okay for Steve and Connie to keep the puppy. What do you think?"

You can decide to continue the discussion, use one of the small group strategies, or introduce a story expansion.

D. Small Group Strategies

1. *Role-Taking:* Set up groups of three or four (or a matching number for the number of characters in the story) and give each student a role to take. For example, Steve, Connie, the apartment manager, and Steve and Connie's mother and father. Give the groups the following instructions:
a. Your group of characters should talk about the best thing for Steve and Connie to do in this situation and why it is the best thing.
b. Remember, use your own ideas about what you believe is right, but discuss these ideas as your character would talk about them. For example, if you think Steve and Connie should keep the puppy, then talk about how the apartment owner might agree that Steve and Connie should keep it.
2. *Illustrating the Ending:* Set up groups of three and give each

group a large piece of drawing paper and crayons. Ask the group to
talk about how the story should end and then make a drawing which
illustrates that ending. Each group can then explain their drawing
to the class, and the teacher can ask probe questions which may promote additional discussion. The other students should also be encouraged to ask questions of the group which is presenting its drawing.

3. *Listing Reasons:* Set up groups of three or four and give them
the following task: List two or three things which you think Steve
and Connie should do because of their problem. Why are these
things good to do? List two or three things which you think they
should *not* do. Why should Steve and Connie not do these?

*Note: A group strategy should always be followed up with a discus-
sion which focuses on what happened in the small groups. At this
point, the teacher can emphasize and provide questions concerning
the reasoning for positions taken during the small group exercises.*

E. Story Expansion

If the initial dilemma story does not create a conflict for the students
or when the students seem to finish a discussion of the initial story,
another aspect may be presented. A story expansion may be thought
of as an additional chapter of the dilemma story.

1. Steve and Connie decide to keep the puppy in the storeroom
for a while. They take good care of the puppy, they bring it food
and water, and stay for several hours each day. One evening, the
apartment building manager knocks on the door of their apartment
and begins talking with Steve and Connie's father. He tells them
that several people have reported to him that Steve and Connie are
keeping a puppy someplace in the building. He wants to know if
this is true and reminds Steve and Connie's father that he has signed
an agreement not to have any pets in the building. If he breaks that
agreement, the family will have to leave the apartment building
within 30 days. The father comes into Connie's room and asks her
if she and Steve have a puppy hidden in the building. The apartment building manager is standing behind the father. Connie doesn't
know what to do. Her father says, "Come on Connie, either you do
or you don't. Please tell me right now."

F. Probe Questions

1. Is it fair for Steve and Connie to bring the puppy into the
apartment building?

2. Should Steve or Connie tell their father about the puppy they
found and are keeping in the storeroom?

3. If Steve or Connie are asked by the manager if they have a dog
hidden in the building, what should they say?

4. The puppy is in the storeroom for a long time, makes such a

mess of things, sometimes barking in the night, that the manager finds out and tells their father. Should Steve and Connie then be punished for breaking the rule?

5. Steve and Connie keep the puppy in the storeroom and tell the manager that they do not have a puppy hidden in the apartment building. Which is worse, breaking the rule or not telling the truth to the building manager?

---

1. What do you think is the central issue of this dilemma?

2. Look at the warm-up questions, the initiating questions, and the probe questions that Galbraith and Jones suggest for this dilemma. Would you suggest any others? Delete any? Why or why not?

3. Would you sequence any of the initiating questions differently? If so, how? And why? What about the warm-up questions or the probe questions?

4. How would you differentiate between dilemmas that are suitable for discussion by elementary students and those suitable for discussion by secondary students?

5. Are there any sorts of issues that you *don't* think elementary-level students should be permitted to discuss? Why or why not?

A CRITIQUE OF THE THEORY [21]

Kohlberg's theory of moral stages is a persuasive one and is appealing to classroom teachers, particularly in its emphasis on movement through the stages being a *natural* process that teachers can further through the discussion of moral dilemmas. Classroom discussion long has been a respected technique engaged in by teachers at all grade levels. However, many people are wary of having teachers and curriculum developers jump too quickly on the moral-stages bandwagon for a number of reasons. What are some of their concerns?

Perhaps the first reservation lies in Kohlberg's argument for the *universality* of the stages. Kohlberg states that the six stages he identified hold for all five of the cultures he examined. However, this is a rather small sample from which to infer the sweeping conclusion that *the* description of moral development for *all* people in *all* cultures has been found. Nor can the sample support the inference that the concept of justice—fundamental to the reasoning inherent in the higher stages (5 and 6)—is endorsed by all cultures. Colin Turnbull, for example, in *The Mountain People,* describes some of the behaviors of the Ik people of northeastern Uganda. The Ik at one time had a peaceful society. They cooperated to hunt for food and honored their dead with burial ceremonies. More recently, the Ugandan government decided to make the

---

[21] Adapted from Jack R. Fraenkel, "The Kohlberg Bandwagon: Some Reservations," *Social Education,* April 1976, pp. 216–222.

Ik's tribal grounds into a national park. It then moved the Ik to a new and very crowded living area on a steep mountainside. As a result of this move the Ik appear to have developed values that are the very antithesis of justice. For example, Turnbull observed a group of them laughing when a young child grabbed a hot coal from a fire and screamed in pain. Young Ik laughed with pleasure as they beat an elderly Ik with sticks and threw stones at him until he cried. An entire village came to the edge of a cliff over which a blind woman had fallen and laughed as she suffered. As a two-year drought destroyed the Ik's crops and starvation set in, hoarding food and keeping it from one's family and from the elders of the tribe became honorable and was viewed as a mark of distinction. Old people were abandoned to die, and burial ceremonies were no longer performed. After living with the Ik for eighteen months, Turnbull summed up his experiences in the following words:

> The IK teach us that our much vaunted human values are not inherent in humanity at all, but are associated only with a particular form of survival called society, and that all, even society itself, are luxuries that can be dispensed with.[22]

As Peters has suggested, Kohlberg and his advocates appear to suffer from the belief that a morality based on the concept of justice is the only type of morality that is defensible.[23] This puts him and his supporters in a somewhat difficult position, for they are forced to defend the proposition that justice is a universally held and admired concept. Unfortunately, there is just too much evidence to the contrary for this to be believed.

A second reservation lies in the assertion that higher-stage reasoning is not only different, but morally *better* than lower-stage reasoning. Such a notion (that "higher" means "better") seems impossible to prove. If higher-stage reasoning is better it should contain or possess something that lower-stage reasoning does not. And if this is true it is difficult to see how those reasoning at the lower stages would be able to understand the arguments of those at the higher stages. And if they cannot understand the arguments, it is difficult to see why those at the lower stages would be inclined to accept such reasoning as better than their own as a justification for various actions. If "higher" is not "better" then there doesn't seem to be any justification for trying to "improve" the reasoning of children by helping them to move through the stages. Michael Scriven argues in a similar vein:

22 Colin Turnbull, *The Mountain People* (New York: Simon & Schuster, 1972).
23 Richard S. Peters, "A Reply to Kohlberg," *Phi Delta Kappan,* June 1975, p. 678.

The put-up or shut-up question [is] whether someone at an "intermediate" stage of moral development is more wrong (or less right) on moral issues than someone at a "higher" stage. If the "lower" stage subjects are not demonstrably wrong, then there's no justification for trying to change them, i.e., for moral education. If they *are* demonstrably wrong, then there must be a proof that they are wrong, i.e., a proof of the increasingly objective nature of the moral standards (or processes) of higher stages; but no satisfactory proof of this has ever been produced . . . Nor is this accidental. If there *were* such a proof, who could undersand it and find it persuasive? Either the lower stages *can* [understand it], in which case it isn't a higher stage proof . . . and should be ignored by truly moral people . . . or the lower stages *can't* understand it, in which case *they* have no good reason to move "upward," in which case *we* have no justification for moving them against their will [or even] thinking they should be moved, since the proof . . . only proves the highest stages are highest to highest stagers. . . . The problem with stage theory, to sum it up, is that a proof that higher means better would either refute stage theory (if every intelligent person could appreciate it) or would be circular—that is, self-refuting or self-serving.[24]

Third, since Kohlberg himself estimates that a majority of people do not get beyond Stage 4, it would seem important to devise ways to get everyone up to and firmly entrenched at this stage. Peters writes:

[Since] few [individuals] are likely to emerge beyond Kohlberg's Stages 3 and 4, it is important that our fellow citizens should be well bedded down at one or the other of these stages. The policeman cannot always be present, and if I am lying in the gutter after being robbed it is somewhat otiose to speculate at what stage the mugger is. My regret must surely be that he had not at least got a conventional morality well instilled in him.[25]

The conventional level (Stages 3 and 4) of reasoning is important for another reason. "[A]t this stage the child learns from the inside, as it were, what it is to follow a rule. Unless he has learned this well (whatever it means!), the notion of following his own rules at the autonomous stage is unintelligible." [26] Before the idea of developing and following one's own rules begins to make any sense, children must understand and appreciate the importance of rules in general for both personal and societal survival. (Can you imagine a society existing without at least some rules?)

24 Michael Scriven, "Cognitive Moral Education," *Phi Delta Kappan,* June 1975, p. 690.
25 Peters, "A Reply to Kohlberg," p. 678.
26 Ibid.

Children also must understand what can happen when rules are disregarded and/or taken lightly by large numbers of people. It certainly is important to realize that rules may be unjust; but the question of *when* and *whether* to disobey an unjust (or any) rule is an important one to explore *explicitly* with children, using a variety of incidents and analogies. We surely do not want to develop a tendency in the young to take rules too lightly or, of course, to view them as inviolate and absolute. This can be avoided only by helping them to realize the value of following rules that at times go against their inclinations. Indeed, a key element of morality, it seems to me, lies in understanding that "resistance to temptation" can be rewarding in its own right. Few specific strategies for developing in children a sense of the importance of rules (and more importantly, a realization that giving in to one's inclinations frequently brings neither happiness nor satisfaction) have yet appeared.

Fourth, the theory places rather unrealistic demands on classroom teachers once they *do* engage students in moral discussions. Kohlberg has stated, "If moral communications are to be effective, the developmental level of the teacher's verbalizations must be one step above the level of the child." [27] If this is true, the requirement presents at least two problems. Since Kohlberg states that only 10 percent of the population reaches Stages 5 or 6, the laws of probability suggest that there are many teachers who themselves reason at the lower stages. They accordingly are likely to come in contact with students who are reasoning at stages higher than their own. Will such teachers be able even to understand, let alone help, such students? How can a teacher who reasons at Stage 3, for example, be expected to present a Stage 5 argument to a Stage 4 student (to foster stage growth) if he or she cannot even understand what such an argument is?

Furthermore, even if enough Stage 5 teachers could be found, they still would face a considerable amount of practical difficulty as they interact with students, no matter what the students' stages may be. Since intellectual development and chronological age are not always the same, most teachers are likely to have children at a variety of stages in their classrooms. It probably would be most unusual, in fact, to find a classroom in which all of the students are at the same stage. Theoretically, at least, this is all to the good, for the divergence of viewpoints would promote more conflict and variety of opinion in class discussions. But Kohlberg argues that children must be exposed to reasoning one level higher than their current stage if development is to be fostered. To do this, a teacher must listen to several responses from each student and figure out what stage of reasoning these responses suggest. The teacher then must either

[27] Lawrence Kohlberg, "The Concepts of Developmental Psychology," p. 42.

frame an appropriate one-stage-higher response during class discussions or mix the students with others who are reasoning one stage higher, so that they may hear their arguments. This seems to be asking an awful lot from busy classroom teachers.

Not all of Kohlberg's supporters appear to agree that children need exposure to reasoning higher than their own. Beyer writes: "Teachers need not be able to identify the stages of reasoning their students use in order to be able to lead moral discussions . . . Teachers who learn to encourage students to respond to each other can usually engage them in arguments at contiguous stages." [28] This statement is rather puzzling. How can a teacher engage students in arguments "at contiguous stages" if he or she can't recognize the stages in the first place? If we take this statement at face value, Beyer appears to be saying, "Don't worry, just engage the students in discussion, and growth in moral reasoning will occur." But he then goes on to say that teachers "with experience and with re-reading reports of Kohlberg's research . . . can become more skilled at identifying the stages at which their students reason." Evidently he himself is not sure how important it is for teachers to be able to locate students at a particular stage. It can't be both ways. Either teachers need to know what the stages are and be able to recognize them when they hear them, or they don't. If they don't, they can forget about stage theory and do what conscientious teachers have done all along—try to engage students in discussions about important issues without specifically trying to expose individuals to the views of those one stage higher. The question remains: Is being able to identify a moral stage important or isn't it?

Fifth, the notion of stages itself is challenged by some scholars. Such social learning psychologists as the Mischels argue that regular changes over time in children's moral judgments may be due simply to the fact that as children grow older, most adults react differently to them. Since parents and other adults talk differently to young children than to adolescents, it should not be surprising that the verbal responses of first and second graders are different than those of teenagers.[29]

Sixth, the argument that all people move through these stages in an invariant sequence has been contradicted by Elizabeth Simpson, who points out that the research to which Kohlberg appeals has demonstrated this only among Stages 2, 3, and 4.[30] Furthermore, in some studies cited by Kohlberg and others, many students showed no stage movement at all.

[28] Barry K. Beyer, "Conducting Moral Discussions," pp. 194–202.
[29] Walter and Harriet Mischel, "A Cognitive Social Learning Approach to Morality and Self-Regulation," in Thomas Likona (ed), *Mortality: Theory, Research, and Social Issues* (New York: Holt, Rinehart & Winston, 1976).
[30] Elizabeth L. Simpson, "Moral Development Research: A Case Study of Scientific Cultural Bias," *Human Development*, 1974, Vol. 17, pp. 81–106.

In Kohlberg's 1969 study, frequently cited as the basis for longitudinal trends in stage movement, just about one-third (32.6 percent) of the students involved showed an overall upward stage change, and only eight of the total sample of forty-three showed one-step upward change.[31] In her 1973 study, Holstein found that only seventeen students of a total sample of fifty-two moved up one stage over a three-year period, with some thirty-three (63.5 percent) showing some general upward movement.[32] And in the Boston and Pittsburgh studies, which Kohlberg describes in his 1975 *Phi Delta Kappan* article, he states that only "about half" of the teachers involved (twenty-four) were able to stimulate upward stage movement. And even that was only from one-quarter to one-half a stage.[33]

As with values clarification, the point of all this is not to discourage teachers and curriculum developers from thinking about stage theory and research. There is much in Kohlberg's work that is extremely interesting and useful. But much of moral development research still is open to question or to alternative interpretation. We should not close our eyes to the fact that Kohlberg's research findings still are mainly hypothesis, calling for further investigation and refinement, rather than statements of established fact.

A CRITIQUE OF SOME EDUCATIONAL SUGGESTIONS BASED ON KOHLBERG'S THEORY

There is no question that the influence of Kohlberg's theory has been considerable. As Rest has mentioned, "Educational programs with such a venerable lineage [Dewey, Piaget, Kohlberg, and so forth], have created interest because of the intellectual heft behind them and the promise of initiating something more than a superficial, piecemeal, short-lived fad." [34] Nevertheless, the manner in which the basic ideas inherent in the theory have been extended into proposals for teaching raises a number of issues and questions that so far have gone unattended by moral reasoning advocates. Let us consider a few of them.

First is what Rest calls "optimal curriculum match." As mentioned earlier, a major goal of education, according to Kohlberg and other developmentalists, is to *stimulate* development through the stages of moral

---

31 Lawrence Kohlberg and R. Kramer, "Continuities and Discontinuities in Childhood and Adult Moral Development," *Human Development*, 1969, pp. 93–120.
32 C. Holstein, "Moral Judgment Change in Early Adolescence and Middle Age: A Longitudinal Study," unpublished paper, 1973.
33 Lawrence Kohlberg, "The Cognitive-Developmental Approach to Moral Education," p. 675.
34 Rest, "Developmental Psychology as a Guide," p. 241.

reasoning. If this can be done, educators would have some very useful information. Rest writes:

> The characterization of the highest stage of development gives a psychological analysis of some competence—e.g., Piaget's stage of formal operations gives us an analysis of what it means to be logical; Kohlberg's "Stage 6" provides a description of what mature moral judgments consists. . . . Note that there is much more specificity here in a characterization of cognitive structure than the honorific labels often used to define educational objectives (such as "creative," "self-actualized," "good-citizen," and "well-adjusted," and so forth).
>
> Furthermore, if the educator has a step-by-step description of the development of some competence, then he has a means of ordering progress (knowing which changes are progressive), of locating people along this course of development, and therefore of anticipating which experiences the student will most likely respond to and from which he will profit. The adage that the teacher should meet the student at the student's level can be given precise and operational meaning if the course of development is defined and the student's level can be assessed. Knowing the course of development enables one to optimize the match between children and curricula and also serves as a guide for sequencing curriculum. Accordingly, at the propitious time, problems that are manageable yet challenging can be introduced to create an interesting learning experience in itself, and, at the same time, to serve to set up the prerequisite components for problems at the next level.[35]

The chief strategy advocated by educators specifically interested in furthering moral development in social studies classrooms, however, is the discussion of moral dilemmas.[36] These dilemmas provoke controversy, and the sorts of questions included in the strategy encourage students to analyze alternatives, though the *explicit* and *sustained* consideration of *consequences* appears minimal. However, these educators do not pay much attention to the notions of optimal curriculum match or curriculum sequencing mentioned by Rest. They do not consider that different kinds of dilemmas may be more profitable (in promoting interest and discussion) at different grade levels or that dilemmas dealing with stage-specific kinds of concerns may be needed to appeal to students reasoning at different stages. They do not discuss the notion of sequencing dilemmas; nor do they consider that one dilemma might be used to build on another so as to further cognitive growth. (The idea of using alternative dilemmas

---

35 Ibid., pp. 243–244.
36 See Galbraith and Jones, *Moral Reasoning;* and Beyer, "Conducting Moral Discussions."

—with the original situation changed to some degree—as a follow-up to the original discussion, however, is a step in this direction.) [37]

At times one gets the uneasy feeling that the advocates of moral discussions have gotten carried away with their own enthusiasm. For example, Beyer makes a number of statements that are either unsupported testimonials ("The most productive discussion involves small group discussions followed by a discussion involving the entire class"); value judgments ("A significant number of students should favor one course of action, while others should favor another"); or unrealistic in what they propose ("After students hear or see the dilemma, the teacher should ask questions in order to help students to clarify the circumstances involved in the dilemma, define terms, identify the characteristics of the central character, and state the exact nature of the dilemma and the action choice open to the central character. *Little more than five minutes* [italics added] need be devoted to this part of the strategy").[38]

Indeed, Beyer's assertion that a program of moral discussions will improve learning skills, self-esteem, and attitudes toward school seems a bit strong for even the converted to swallow whole. No evidence is provided to support this sweeping claim. Why should participating in a moral discussion (or in any discussion, for that matter) *ipso facto* help students to develop listening skills or to improve their self-esteem? Discussions can be conducted poorly or well; the mere assertion of their value does not improve a person's skills or change his or her attitudes. It would seem more likely that the manner in which a discussion is conducted would be the crucial factor.

A word, too, is in order about the nature of the dilemmas themselves. Some of those that I have seen and that are cited by Kohlberg, Fenton, Beyer, Galbraith, and others are either narrow in scope (for example, "Should Jill give Sharon's name to the Security Officer?"), or affect only one or a few individuals (e.g., "Should a Christian girl in Nazi Germany break the law and jeopardize her family by hiding her Jewish friend from the Gestapo?"). This is apparently intentional. Beyer states that a moral dilemma "should be as simple as possible. The dilemma should involve only a few characters in a relatively uncomplicated situation which students can grasp readily. Complicated dilemmas confuse students who are then forced to spend time clarifying facts and circumstances rather than discussing reasons for suggested actions." [39]

This sort of assertion can be debated on a number of counts. First, dilemmas in real life are rarely simple. Second, students need exposure to a wide variety of issues and dilemmas as they move through the grades, particularly to those that can affect the lives of many people. Thus can

[37] Galbraith and Jones, *Moral Reasoning*, p. 19.
[38] Beyer, "Conducting Moral Discussions."
[39] Ibid.

they become aware of the sorts of problems that exist in the real world. (For example, "Should the President of the United States 'send in the marines' against the oil-producing nations if they will not supply us with oil?") Third, how are students to learn to sort out and analyze the facts involved in the complicated issues they will face in real life if they get little practice doing so in schools? Such issues include abortion, taxation, local control of schools, euthanasia, busing, drug usage, environmental contamination, the right of public employees to strike, and so on. Fourth, students *need* practice (and lots of it) in "clarifying facts and circumstances" if they are to find out about the nature of their world.

The notion of sequencing dilemmas in some fashion seems in order here. One possibility would be to make the dilemmas increasingly more complex, abstract, and difficult as students progress through the grades. Such a scheme might entail presenting students in the elementary grades with fairly simple, interpersonal and intrapersonal conflicts revolving around such concepts as fairness, reward, punishment, responsibility, authority, and conscience. As students move into junior and senior high school, they could at each grade level be presented with dilemmas involving larger and larger groups of people, including governments and international agencies. Such dilemmas, not only interpersonal but also intergovernmental and global (involving more than two governments), could focus on such additional concepts as honor, duty, contract, property, civil liberties, and obligation. This might be one way of providing more breadth to the types of dilemmas presented to students, while promoting the more fundamental, long-term, and cumulative change concerning developmentalists.

It also should be pointed out that the strategy for guiding moral discussions suggested by Kohlberg's supporters [40] is only one of many possibilities. The steps these authors present do offer some concrete ideas for starting a moral discussion in the classroom, but this is not the "one and only" way to go about the matter. Other models [41] *do* exist, and teachers can be encouraged to create their own strategies and models when and where appropriate.

Furthermore, we are not even sure that it is the discussion of the dilemmas themselves that brings about stage movement. It certainly is conceivable that a sensitive and concerned teacher—one who continually engages students in conversation and asks them questions and lets them know by comments and actions that he or she is interested in what they have to say—may be the independent variable in this regard. The dis-

---

40 See Ibid.
41 See Maurice P. Hunt and Lawrence E. Metcalf, *Teaching High School Social Studies* (New York: Harper & Row, 1968), p. 134, and Jack R. Fraenkel, *Helping Students Think and Value: Strategies for Teaching the Social Studies* (Englewood Cliffs, N.J.: Prentice-Hall, 1973), p. 266.

cussion of moral dilemmas may be irrelevant. Perhaps the discussion of nonmoral, controversial issues would do just as well. At this point, we just don't know.

More than anything else, the discussion of moral dilemmas seems a very limiting sort of strategy to recommend. In the first place, discussion does not work very well or for very long with children below the age of ten or so. You simply can't have much of an intellectual discussion with third and fourth graders. Such other ways of presenting information about moral relationships and dilemmas as the use of models and concrete examples must be used. Second, the use of case studies, which is what moral dilemmas are, focuses on specific instances rather than on general principles. This often presents a problem in that only a few children in the class consider the particular case interesting or applicable to them. However, an emphasis on more general principles (for example, that one often must make exceptions to rules) allows reference to a large number of examples by both teacher and students. This increases the interest and involvement of the whole class.[42] Finally, the likelihood of several *different* types of alternative suggestions being proposed by a class of students reasoning at Stages 2 or 3 (where many educators say most high school students are likely to be) [43] does not seem very great. A more appropriate strategy would be to encourage teachers (and curriculum developers and publishers) not only to present dilemmas in interesting and exciting ways and in a variety of formats (printed, oral, visual), but also to present a range of alternative solutions (at various stage levels) for *resolving* those dilemmas. In discussing the dilemma, the teacher then could include a systematic consideration of the various alternatives. This would not in any way preclude students from suggesting their own alternatives in addition to those presented. I am struck by Clive Beck's notion that perhaps one reason a lot of people do not develop morally is because better alternatives have not occurred to them. They frequently continue to react in conventional ways, because they perceive no other way of reacting. The above suggestion would, in Beck's words, "extend their imagination." [44]

---

1. Consider again the criticisms of the moral reasoning approach I have proposed on pages 71–80. Do you find them legitimate? Persuasive? Why or why not?

[42] Clive Beck, "The Development of Moral Judgment," in James A. Phillips, Jr., (ed.), *Developing Value Constructs in Schooling: Inquiry into Process and Product* (Worthington, Ohio: Ohio Association for Supervision and Curriculum Development, 1972), p. 45.
[43] See Beyer, "Conducting Moral Discussions," p. 201; and Edwin Fenton, "Moral Education: The Research Findings," *Social Education*, April 1976, p. 191.
[44] Beck, "The Development of Moral Judgment," p. 44.

2. Like values clarification, the moral reasoning approach has had a considerable impact on many curriculum developers and teachers, particularly those who work in the social studies. How would you account for its popularity? Is such popularity justified? Why or why not?

3. On balance would you say the strengths of this approach overshadow the weaknesses, or vice versa? Why?

4. What other weaknesses and/or strengths of this approach do you perceive?

5. Which (if either) do you think offers the greatest promise for use with elementary students—values clarification or the discussion of moral dilemmas? Why? Which do you think offers the greatest promise for use with secondary students? Why?

6. What suggestions would you make for combining the two approaches?

EXERCISES

1. Try out one of the dilemmas on page 61 or 65 and their alternatives with some people you know. What sorts of actions do people suggest? What levels of moral reasoning do you find? Is it easy to get a discussion going with these dilemmas? Why or why not?

2. Here are a number of statements concerning Helga's dilemma (pages 61–62) that Galbraith and Jones place at different levels of moral development.[45] At what stage would you place each statement?

  a. "Helga has an obligation to her family. She will really let them down if she gets them all in trouble."

  b. "Helga shouldn't let her in, because Rachel probably wouldn't let Helga in if she got into trouble with the Gestapo."

  c. "Friendship is not the issue. If Helga was really concerned about the problem in her society, she should be helping all the Jews in order to protest the government action. She should not hide Rachel unless she intends to hide other Jews and to make a public protest in opposition to putting Jews in concentration camps."

  d. "If Helga lets Rachel in she might also get in trouble with the Gestapo."

  e. "Helga has an obligation to obey the laws of her society."

Look at the stage identification of these statements by Galbraith and Jones listed on page 82. Would you agree with their placement?

3. Look at some of the statements public officials use to justify some of their decisions, as reported in the daily press. What levels of moral reasoning do they suggest?

4. Listed below is a statement written by Martin Luther King, Jr., while he was in jail in Birmingham, Alabama. It is one of the few statements available that Kohlberg has placed at Stage 6. Show the statement

---

45 In *Social Education,* January 1975, p. 20.

to a number of individuals, and ask them if they agree with it or not and why. Based on their responses, what conclusions would you draw about the stage of moral reasoning of most people?

> There is a type of constructive nonviolent tension which is necessary for growth. Just as Socrates felt it was necessary to create a tension in the mind so that individuals could rise from the bondage of half-truths, so must we see the need for nonviolent gadflies to create the kind of tension in society that will help men rise from the dark depths of prejudice and racism.
>
> One may well ask, "How can you advocate breaking some laws and obeying others?" The answer lies in the fact that there are two types of laws, just and unjust. One has not only a legal but a moral responsibility to obey just laws. One has a moral responsibility to disobey unjust laws. An unjust law is a human law that is not rooted in eternal law and natural law. Any law that uplifts human personality is just, any law that degrades human personality is unjust. An unjust law is a code that a numerical or power majority group compels a minority group to obey but does not make binding on itself.[46]

5. Present the two stories on pp. 53–54 to children between the ages of five and seven, seven and eleven, and eleven and fifteen. Ask them to state which child they think is the naughtier and why. What differences do you notice in their evaluations as to which of the two children is the naughtiest? How do the reasons they give to explain their choice differ? Do the responses you obtain support Piaget's distinctions as presented in Table 1 on page 53?

Galbraith and Jones Stage Identification

Stage 1: "If Helga lets Rachel in she might also get into trouble with the Gestapo."

Stage 2: "Helga shouldn't let her in because Rachel probably wouldn't let Helga in if she got into trouble with the Gestapo."

Stage 3: "Helga has an obligation to her family. She will really let them down if she gets them all in trouble."

Stage 4: "Helga has an obligation to obey the laws of her society."

Stage 5: "Friendship is not the issue. If Helga was really concerned about the problem in her society, she should be helping all the Jews in order to protest the government action. She should not hide Rachel unless she intends to hide other Jews and to make a public protest in opposition to putting Jews in concentration camps."

---

[46] Martin Luther King, Jr., "Letter from a Birmingham Jail," in *Why We Can't Wait,* © 1963 by Martin Luther King, Jr. By permission of Harper & Row, Publishers.

chapter five

MAKING INFERENCES ABOUT VALUES

The work of Kohlberg and Raths and their supporters provides us with considerable food for thought about what a school program of values education should include. Clearly, the development of a child's ability to think rationally about moral issues is an important task for teachers to pursue. So, too, is the clarification of a student's personal commitments. It seems only logical to assert that both these objectives should be an integral part of any values education program, for children must develop both intellectually and emotionally if they are to become fully functioning and psychologically whole human beings. Indeed, as was mentioned in Chapter 1, it is becoming more and more clear that intellectual and emotional development are interdependent. That is, people may fail to grasp the meaning of something because they lack emotional sensitivity; but they also may be insensitive, because they lack the intellectual understanding of how people feel. To the extent that the discussion of moral dilemmas or participation in values clarification activities contributes to the intellectual and/or emotional development of students, their use is only to be encouraged.

But is an emphasis on moral reasoning and values clarification enough? Should the discussion of moral dilemmas and the clarification of personal commitments be considered the equivalent of values education? In my opinion, they should not, for there are some additional procedures and strategies that any comprehensive program of values education should include. In this chapter and the next are some suggestions as to what some of these procedures and strategies might be. In particular, in this chapter are some ways to help students identify, compare, and contrast values. Chapter 6 includes some ways to help them analyze values and value judgments and to explore feelings.[1]

THE IMPORTANCE OF A RATIONALE

In Chapter 1 it was suggested that values education goes on all the time in schools. Teachers teach values, at least implicitly, every day. Both the formal and the informal, "hidden," curricula are loaded with values. Assignments, statements, questions, discussion topics, examinations—all reflect what a teacher values. Somewhat less obviously, administrative announcements, the school budget, faculty loads, the school grounds, buildings, counselor recommendations, holidays, student government, school district policies—these too reflect values.

Two key questions for teachers to ask themselves, however, are whether they are teaching the values they *want* to teach and whether the values they want to teach are *worth teaching*. Administrators might ask themselves what values their schools reflect and whether these are the values they want reflected. You might do the same. What kinds of individuals would you want the schools to develop? In what kind of world do you want them to live? What knowledge and skills do you think students will need in the future to sustain themselves and their society, or when necessary, to change it? What kinds of assignments would (do) you give? In what kinds of activities would you have students participate? What kinds of books, movies, plays, and so on would you recommend? What topics would you discuss? What questions would you ask? Why?

More generally, what do you consider important in life? What kinds of books do you read? What about magazines and newspapers? What kinds of music and art do you like? How do you feel about politicians, sports, big business, religion, education, other people, other countries, world government? What do you think should be done about crime, poverty, the environment, overpopulation, drugs, urban decay, traffic congestion, alienation, foreign policy? What kinds of government policies would you recommend toward the aged, the poor, the sick, the disabled? What should the schools do with regard to these groups? What do you like and dislike? Would you want to teach your students to like what you like? To value what you value?

Formulating, analyzing, and justifying answers to such questions as

[1] Much of the material in this chapter and the next has been adapted from Jack R. Fraenkel, "Teaching About Values" in Carl Ubbelohde and Jack R. Fraenkel, (eds.), *Values and the American Heritage*, 46th Yearbook of the National Council for the Social Studies (Washington, D.C.: NCSS, 1976), Part II, pp. 164–207.

these often is referred to as developing a *rationale*. It is not an easy task, but it is a very important one for all teachers to attempt. Shaver and Strong offer some reasons why:

> The question . . . is not *whether* you will deal with values or *whether* your values will affect what you do. It is rather, *what* will you do about values, and *will you be aware* of the influence of your own values and make it as conscious and rational as possible? . . . If your behavior as a teacher is to be as rational as possible, [then your unexplicated, unexamined] assumptions need to be brought into the open, stated as clearly as possible, examined for accuracy and consistency, and used as the basis for decisions about your instructional and other behavior toward students . . . The product of this process of explicating and clarifying one's frame of reference we call a *rationale*. Defined more precisely, a rationale is the statement and explication of the basic principles upon which your school behavior (both in the formal classroom setting and during the encounters within the school's social and political system) is based.
>
> The development of an explicit rationale for teaching, as distinct from a largely implicit frame of reference, is essential but not easy. Among the areas needing clarification are your assumptions about society and the school's relationship to it, about the nature of children and how they learn, about the nature of values. The critical examination of your unconscious and frequently cherished assumptions in these areas is not something that you will accomplish overnight, or even during an undergraduate course or an inservice training program. In fact, you are not likely ever to arrive at a completely explicated and polished rationale.
>
> A rationale, like the person who is attempting to develop it, evolves and is always in the process of becoming. Your rationale may become more explicit, more comprehensive, more logical in the interrelationship of its parts, clearer in its implications for your behavior as a teacher. But it ought never to be considered final, for that would imply that you have stopped changing and growing.
>
> One important reason for developing a rationale is to avoid the unthinking imposition of your beliefs on your students. Equally important from a pragmatic point of view is the need for a systematic, well-grounded basis from which to explain, even defend, your instructional behavior to administrators and parents. . . .
>
> When schooling touches on values, parents are particularly likely to react emotionally. For that reason, any teacher who decides to deal with values explicitly (recognizing, of course, that no teacher can avoid dealing with values implicitly) ought to have a conscious rationale as a foundation for his or her approach. Communication of this rationale to other teachers, to the principal, and even to the superintendent, may help to insure that vital support will be avail-

able if needed. Moreover, going through the process of discussing your rationale with other school people may help you to communicate it later to parents and to persuade them of its soundness.[2]

When it comes to values, then, a rationale is important for teachers to develop for a number of reasons. It can help them to clarify their own values. It can help them to decide what values they want to teach and why and to explain the reasons for their decision to others. It can help them to choose from among the often conflicting procedures that advocates of differing approaches to values education recommend. It can help them to select appropriate value-oriented subject matter and learning activities for students. And perhaps most importantly, it can help them to determine what values are worth teaching in the first place.

---

1. What values do you find reflected in this argument for developing a rationale?

2. Do you think most teachers have a rationale for what they teach and how they teach? If not, why not?

3. "The development of an explicit rationale for teaching . . . is essential but not easy." Would you agree? Why or why not?

4. Teachers are frequently encouraged to be clear about their *objectives* or *goals*. In what ways, if any, are goals and objectives different from a rationale?

QUESTIONS THAT FOCUS ON VALUES

The essence of any investigation or exploration of values lies in the questions a teacher asks. All questions, of course, help to get students to think. But different purposes dictate different questions. Depending on what a teacher wants to find out (or help students to find out), different kinds of questions need to be asked. Certain kinds of questions, however, are more likely to involve values than others.

Some examples of three categories of questions that teachers can ask to help students make inferences about and engage in discussions of values follow. The three categories are:

- Questions that ask for facts.
- Questions that ask for definitions.
- Questions that ask for inferences.

These categories differ primarily in terms of the purposes behind them and the types of responses they are likely to evoke.

2 James P. Shaver and William Strong, *Facing Value Decisions: Rationale-Building for Teachers* (Belmont, Calif.: Wadsworth Publishing Co., 1976), pp. 6–8.

"I wish I at least knew enough about something
to ask questions."

Source: Reg Hider from *Today's Education,* December 1971, p. 61. Reprinted by permission of National Education Association.

Questions That Ask for Facts

The chief purpose of factual-type questions is to determine if students have acquired or obtained a desired amount of factual data. Here are some examples:

Who was the author of *A Tale of Two Cities?*
What territory did the United States purchase from France in 1803?
When was the Peace Corps established?
Where is the country of Chad located?
How does a volcano develop?
In what order did the thirteen Colonies ratify the Bill of Rights?
In what play do the characters Rosencrantz and Guildenstern appear?
What is the volume of this cube?

Notice that factual-type questions ask students to make assertions about the observable world and about things, events, or individuals within it. These assertions are ultimately verifiable by recourse to *observation.* The truth or falsity of a student's response to a factual-type question lies in the presence or absence of publicly observable evidence. This evidence indicates that the thing(s), event(s), or individual(s) to which

Source: © King Features Syndicate, Inc. 1974.

the student refers does or did exist or that it is (they are) happening or did happen. (For example, there either was or was not an individual named Charles Dickens who wrote a book entitled *A Tale of Two Cities*.)

Questions That Ask for Definitions

The main purpose of definitional-type questions is to find out what someone means when he or she uses a given term or phrase.
Here are some examples:

> What do you mean by "patriotic"?
> Can you give me an example?
> What characteristics must a thing possess to qualify as a "hexagon"?

To answer this type of question, students must either give an example of or describe the essential characteristics of something. Note that there is no such thing as a "correct" answer to a definitional-type question—only more-or-less "agreed-on" answers. When students offer a definition, they are not describing a state of affairs or the occurrence of an event or happening. They are not saying something about the nature of the real world but instead something about the meaning of words. The acceptability of a response to a definitional-type question lies in the degree to which the student's definition agrees with an official or authoritative one found in a recognized source such as a dictionary. If the word being defined does not appear in a dictionary, the acceptability of the definition depends on the degree to which it is clear and promotes the understanding of those with whom the word is being used.

Questions That Ask for Inferences

Inferential-type questions ask students to "go beyond the data" previously acquired, to explain why they think something happened, to draw a conclusion, to suggest an attitude, a feeling, a value, or a state of mind, or to form a hypothesis about what might happen sometime in the future. Here are some examples:

What caused him to do that?
How did Sam feel?
What else might Alice do?
What conclusion can you draw from all this?
What would you say Mrs. Thompson considers important?
If she did that, what might happen?

Here many answers, all equally acceptable, are possible. There is no such thing as "the" or even "a" correct answer to inferential-type questions. Students are asked to do such things as: (1) to reflect on and analyze facts, (2) to explain possible relationships that they think exist among facts, (3) to identify feelings and values, or (4) to "make a reasoned guess" as to how something will turn out. Notice that all questions that ask students to identify values are inferential-type questions (see Figure 5-1).

QUESTIONING PATTERNS

It is not only the questions a teacher asks that are important in getting students to make inferences about values but also *how* they are

Factual-type questions ask for:	Definitional-type questions ask for:	Inferential-type questions ask for:
Names	Characteristics	Conclusions
Dates	Examples	Alternatives
Places	Meanings	Generalizations
Events		Values
Descriptions		Feelings
		Hypotheses

FIGURE 5-1 *Types of responses called for by different categories of questions.*

asked. A criticism of values clarification advocates (that also would apply to moral reasoning supporters) made earlier (see pages 46–47) was that they do not stress, or even make clear, the importance of *facts* to intelligent decision making. As a result, they have not built any procedures for encouraging and helping students to engage in systematic fact gathering into their activities and strategies. They apparently fail to realize that intelligent inferences and decisions about values are unlikely if students do not understand the *facts* involved in value incidents and dilemmas.

I would argue, however, that a foundation of factual data—a data bank of facts, so to speak—needs to be acquired *before* students are asked to make inferences about values or to discuss moral dilemmas. Also, questions that ask students to search for factual information usually should be asked before questions about values if value discussions are to prosper. One exception, however, might be that inferential type questions sometimes might be asked before a discussion begins in order to interest students—that is, to motivate them.

Two sorts of questioning patterns, therefore, suggest themselves. The first, called *horizontal extending,* is used when a teacher desires to evoke more of the *same type of response* from students. For example, a teacher wanting more facts to come out continues to ask factual-type questions of several students *before* asking any other type of question. If more inferences of why the facts occurred are desired the teacher continues to ask questions that call for inferences about reasons. The same applies to any other type of question that might be asked. The *same type* of question is asked again and again before moving on to a different type. In the example below, a teacher has just shown her class a film describing the contrasting life styles and occupations of two men—a youth worker and an automobile mechanic. In the film, the two individuals are interviewed concerning what they like about their jobs. The teacher wants to make sure that all her students understand what each man did and said *before* she asks them to make inferences about the men's values. She proceeds as follows:

Teacher: All right, what can you tell me about the youth worker we saw in the film? Remember, I'm interested in what you observed about this man, not what you think of him.

Al: He doesn't work any definite, set number of hours in a day.

Joe: And he spends a lot of his leisure time with kids.

Teacher: What else can you tell me?

Sue: He's single.

Bob: He's the coach of a Little League team.

Teacher: What else did the film show about him?

Phil: He takes kids lots of places, like the zoo and horseback riding.

Al: He's a keen guy.

Teacher: Did the film show you that, Al, or is that your impression?

Al: My impression.

Teacher: Okay, but right now let's try to zero in on what the film showed us about this youth worker. Now, what else did you observe about him? . . .

The teacher in this instance is seeking to obtain from her class as many facts as she can regarding the people in the film. Therefore, she repeatedly asks *only* questions that call for factual information. Her purpose in doing so is to get as many facts of the situation identified and recorded as possible. Thus, there will be a sizable base of information available from which students can make inferences. Once she has obtained as many facts as judgment tells her she is likely to get she can proceed to ask a series of questions that call for inferences about reasons. When she has acquired a fair number of such inferences, she can ask a series of questions that call for inferences about values. These questions call for students to suggest similarities and differences, to form conclusions, and so on. Figure 5-2 illustrates this pattern of horizontal extending, and Figure 5-3 is the chart that eventually resulted from the discussion of the film.

A second type of pattern is that of *vertical extending*. This pattern is used when a teacher wishes to obtain a different kind of response after having obtaining several responses of the same type. For example, when a teacher *asks the same student* a factual-type question followed by one

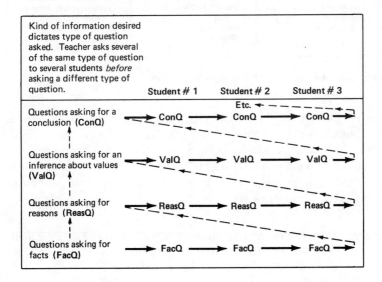

FIGURE 5-2   Horizontal extending.

		INFERENCES
FACTS	REASONS	VALUES
Youth Worker Employed by 4-H. Runs youth program. Takes kids riding. Holds team practices. Has no definite hours. Exposes kids to new experiences. Spends leisure time with kids. Is single.	Doesn't want kids to suffer. Likes kids to have new experiences. Personal satisfaction. Wants to make a contribution. Enjoys kids. Wants to improve skills. Trying to give himself happy childhood. Likes to be important. Wants to be a big brother. Maybe had a youth leader.	Teamwork. Kids. Contribution to community. Exposure (lots of experience). Being unselfish. People over time. Physical comfort. Purpose in life. Contact comfort. Escaping adult world.
Mechanic Works 8 to 5. Takes motors apart. Races cars as a hobby. Married, has family. Works with tools. Checks out cars. Defines success in terms of family and car. Son helps him before race. Travels 180 m.p.h. Is sponsored by Rosenthal.	Needs excitement. Wants approval, to feel important. Wants to win. Enjoys working with hands. Death wish. Gets away from family. Not ready to grow up. Earns extra money. Wants to be popular. Doesn't know anything else. Pay is good. What he is good at. Promotes business.	Power. Fame. Speed. Pride in work. Machines. Neatness. Achievement. Success. Family. Money. Being "above" people. Using leisure at what he knows. Showing off for family.

FIGURE 5-3 An example of a completed values information chart.

asking for inferences about reasons, followed with one asking for inferences about values, he or she is engaging in vertical extension with that student. This pattern usually is followed when a teacher wishes to have a student or class make inferences and draw conclusions about a *particular* fact rather than produce a large number of facts and inferences for charting. Here is an example:

Teacher: Who can name an explorer who sailed from Europe during the fifteenth century? Doris? (Asking for facts.)

Doris: Columbus?

Teacher: Okay. Why did Columbus sail at that time, Doris? (Asking for inferences about reasons.)

Doris: He was trying to find a new route to the East Indies.

Teacher: What does that suggest about him? (Asking for a simple conclusion.)

Doris: I don't know. Maybe that he was curious?

Teacher: All right. Who can name another explorer from that time? Al? (Asking for facts.)

Al: Ponce de Leon.

Teacher: Why did he sail, do you think? (Asking for inferences about reasons.)

Al: He was looking for the fountain of youth, which a lot of people believed in then.

Teacher: What's that suggest about him? (Asking for a conclusion.)

Al: He was a product of his time, I guess.

Notice that each of the questions this teacher asks is of a different type than the one that precedes it. Also notice that she asks one of each type of each student before going on to another student.[3] Figure 5-4 illustrates this pattern.

In my experience, horizontal extension is a more profitable pattern to pursue when it comes to initiating and maintaining classroom discussions about values. This is particularly true when one wishes to obtain a

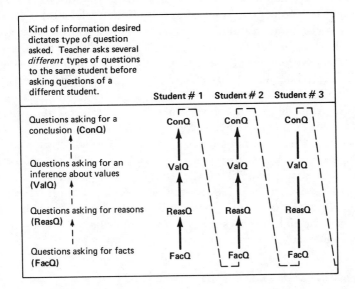

FIGURE 5-4 Vertical extending.

[3] Questions that ask for definitions are asked in both patterns whenever the meaning of a word is unclear and the teacher (or a student) deems it necessary to have the word defined.

values chart containing a sizable amount of information. Also, the discussions that ensue are more likely to involve more students participating at the same level (i.e., more discussing reasons, inferences, and so on at the same time). On the other hand, if a teacher wants to zero in on a particular student and help him extend his thinking in some depth, then vertical extension seems appropriate. But it is a good idea to try both patterns to determine the strengths and weaknesses of each as far as your own teaching style is concerned.

---

1. Which type of question—factual, definitional, or inferential—do you think is most important? Why? Which type do you think is the easiest for students to answer? (Check this out. Ask a number of people some questions from each of the three categories described on pages 87–89, and see which kind they have the most trouble answering.)

2. Would you agree that a foundation of factual information should be acquired before students are asked to make any inferences about values? Why or why not?

3. What other patterns of questioning besides horizontal and vertical extending can you suggest?

IDENTIFYING VALUES

With these different types of questions and questioning patterns in mind, consider now a questioning strategy that teachers can use to help students make some reasoned inferences about a person's (or group's) values. The essence of the strategy involves presenting students with a *value incident,* then asking them to suggest what values the incident reflects. A value incident is a statement, argument, description, or illustration in which an individual or group does or says something that indicates or implies what he, she, or they thinks is important in life. Charts are used to record student responses for later analysis.

Value incidents can be found in a variety of different sources including newspaper and magazine articles, excerpts from fiction, political cartoons, comic strips, advertisements, editorials, essays, poems, even songs. Some examples of such incidents were presented in Chapter 2 (see pages 16–23). Here are two more, both suitable for use with older (upper junior high or high school) students. Notice that both illustrate or imply the recommendation of something.

Example #1: A Poem [4]

I knew this skinny little kid
Who never wanted to play tackle football at all

[4] James Kavanaugh, "I Knew This Kid," in *Will You Be My Friend?* (Los Angeles: Nash Publishing Co., 1971).

But thought he'd better if he wanted
His daddy to love him and to prove his courage
And things like that.
I remember him holding his breath
And closing his eyes
And throwing a block into a guy twice his size,
Proving he was brave enough to be loved, and crying softly
Because his tailbone hurt.
And his shoes were so big they made him stumble.

I knew this skinny little kid
With sky-blue eyes and soft brown hair
Who liked cattails and pussy willows,
Sumac huts and sassafras,
Who liked chestnuts and pine cones and oily walnuts,
Lurking foxes and rabbits munching lilies,
Secret caves and moss around the roots of oaks,
Beavers and muskrats and gawking herons.
And I wonder what he would have been
If someone had loved him for
Just following the fawns and building waterfalls
And watching the white rats have babies.
I wonder what he would have been
If he hadn't played tackle football at all.

Example #2: An Autobiographical Statement [5]

One day I was standing in the front part of the store, waiting for the next customer. A man came in and asked me if we had any high, tan shoes. I told him that we had no shoes of that style. He thanked me and walked out of the store. The floorwalker came up to me and asked me what the man wanted. I told him what the man asked for and what I replied. The floorwalker said angrily: "Damn it! We're not here to sell what they want. We're here to sell what we've got." He went on to instruct me that when a customer came into the store, the first thing to do was to get him to sit down and take off his shoe so that he couldn't get out of the store. "If we don't have what he wants," he said, "bring him something else and try to interest him in that style. If he is still uninterested, inform the floorwalker and he will send one of the regular salesmen, and if that doesn't work, a third salesman will be sent to him. Our policy is that no customer gets out of the store without a sale until at least three salesmen have worked on him. By that time he feels that he must be a crank and will generally buy something whether he wants it or not."

I learned from other clerks that if a customer needed a 7-B shoe and we did not have that size in the style he desired, I should try on an 8-A or 7-C or some other size. The sizes were marked in code

[5] From *White Collar Crime* by Edward H. Sutherland. Copyright, 1949, by Holt, Rinehart and Winston, Inc. Reprinted by permission of Holt, Rinehart and Winston.

so that the customer did not know what the size was, and it might be necessary to lie to him about the size; also his foot might be injured by the misfit. But the rule was to sell him a pair of shoes, preferably a pair that fit but some other pair if necessary.

I learned also that the clerks received an extra commission if they sold out-of-style shoes left over from earlier seasons, which were called "spiffs." The regular salesmen made a practice of selling spiffs to anyone who appeared gullible and generally had to claim either that this was the latest style or that it had been the style earlier and was coming back this season, or that it was an old style but much better quality than present styles. The clerk had to size up the customer and determine which one of these lies would be most likely to result in a sale.

Here is yet another example, one more suitable for use with elementary students.

Example #3: An Excerpt from a Textbook [6]

Twelve-year-old Marcia Brandon is waging a one-girl drive for government action. She wants to save a pond.

The pond in Marcia's neighborhood is to be filled in to make land for a new county hospital. Marcia claims that the pond is a resting place for waterbirds. She also says that the whole area would be better as a park. This would save the pond and give children in the area a place to play.

Marcia began her drive by writing to the mayor of her city. But the mayor's office said the new hospital was a county building and the land was owned by the state. Marcia then wrote to the county board and to her city's representative at the state capital. She also sent a letter to a government office in Washington, D.C. She hoped that the government there might help by making the pond a wildlife preserve.

The newspapers became aware of Marcia's efforts the following week. It was then that she started a door-to-door drive for signatures. She hoped that if enough people signed their names, the building plans would be changed.

The three examples above are only a few of many different types of value incidents that might be suggested. The key characteristic that all value incidents have in common is that they represent instances in which an individual does or says something that suggests what he or she considers worthwhile—that is, worth having or doing or trying to attain. In

---

[6] David C. King and Charlotte C. Anderson, *The United States* (Boston: Houghton-Mifflin Co., 1976), p. 124.

short, what the person values. This is obviously a crucial characteristic, for students cannot be expected to make inferences about a person's values if the incident they witness does not show that person doing or saying something that reflects his or her values.

After the value incident has been read (or looked at, listened to, and so on), the teacher (or another student) asks the class several questions about the incident in a predetermined sequence. The class is encouraged to analyze the incident in terms of the values they think it reflects. The questioner's task is to:

- Ask for facts.
- Ask for inferences about reasons why the facts occurred.
- Ask for inferences about what the individual values.
- Ask for specific evidence to support the inferences.

Here is one set of questions organized along these lines.

1. What is this (story, editorial, cartoon) about?/What is happening in this incident?
2. What do you think are the main character's reasons for saying or doing this?
3. What do these reasons suggest to you about what is important to this individual? Why?

Students should be encouraged to suggest as many different possibilities as they can in response to questions 2 and 3. As students seek to answer the questions, it is often helpful to prepare a *values information chart* on the blackboard (or in student notebooks) as shown in Figure 5-5.

Once the chart contains a sizable amount of information (the more the better), the class can be asked to *focus* on the third column of the chart and then discuss the following questions.

4. Why do you suppose people consider _____ (choose a particular value here from the third column) important?
5. Would you endorse such a value yourself?

What happened?	Why we think it happened.	What this suggests the individual (s) involved consider important.
FACTS	REASONS	VALUES

FIGURE 5-5 A values information chart.

Each of these questions is asked for a particular purpose. Question 1 asks students to identify the acts and/or words of an individual in a particular situation that involves that individual's values. Questions 2 and 3 ask a class to infer the reasons for and values underlying this behavior. Notice that there are "correct" answers to question 1, but not to questions 2 and 3. The teacher should take great pains to encourage any and all responses to these questions. Question 4 then encourages students to think about why people value what they do.

A special remark must be made about question 5; it is *not* a question to be debated. It is a question calling for a show of personal commitment on the part of the student. The teacher should accept all student responses here, no matter what they might be. And any and all students have the right to answer or not to answer this question.

---

1. The major purpose behind this strategy is to help students make reasoned inferences about the values of other people. With this objective in mind, take a look again at the questions asked as part of the strategy. Would you recommend asking any additional questions? Deleting any? If so, why?

2. Would you agree that question 5 is indeed "not a question to be debated"? Why or why not? Are there any conditions under which you might wish to debate this question? If so, when?

3. Are there any types of value incidents that you would *not* want students to consider? Why or why not?

4. Should students be *encouraged* to make inferences about the values of their teachers? The values of other students? Are there any individuals about which inferences as to their values should be discouraged? If so, why?

COMPARING AND CONTRASTING VALUES

The assumption underlying the previous set of questions is that teachers can use them to help students make reasoned inferences about what other people value. A single incident, however, is a very shaky foundation upon which to base an inference about another person's values. Asking students to look for indications of values in a particular instance is helpful in alerting them to the fact that actions and words are value indicators. We can be mistaken, however, for the individual(s) involved may be trying to confuse or mislead us. Or they may be acting under duress or unusual stress. They may be acting a certain way out of fear or ignorance. The idea of *consistency of actions over time* therefore is an important concept for students to understand and think about. It is helpful to encourage students to follow the words and actions of a given individual over time (for example, those of a public official as reported in the press and other media). What contradictions do they notice? In what way(s) would they modify their original conclusions? And why?

What *specific evidence* caused them to modify previous conclusions? A focus on evidence for any conclusion is crucial, since it helps students to see that conclusions vary in terms of how warranted they are. Attention to the amount of evidence available to support or refute a conclusion, therefore, should be continual.

Figure 5-6 presents a skeleton of a chart that can be used to compare an individual's statements and actions over time as well as differing conclusions by students about the individual's values. Along the top are entered the things to be compared (that is, different sayings or actions of the same individual at different times). The questions to be asked are in the left-hand column.

Figure 5-6 is designed to help students investigate how the same person's words and actions hold up over time. But teachers also can help students to consider what *different* people do or say in the same situation —again by asking students a set of predetermined questions in a given order. In this case, the questioner:

- Asks for facts. (That is, what did an individual do or say in a particular situation?)
- Asks for reasons. (Why did he or she do this?)
- Asks for inferences about what the individual values.
- Asks for specific evidence that supports the inferences.

This information can be recorded on a retrieval chart kept individually by students in their notebooks or jointly on a bulletin board or black-

Questions	First action or saying	Second action or saying	Third action or saying	Etc.
What happened? (Facts)				
Why did it happen? (Reasons)				
What does the person (s) or group (s) consider important? (Values)				

FIGURE 5-6 *Comparing and contrasting the values of the same individual in different situations.*

board. Students then are asked the same questions about another individual involved in the same situation or in a similar situation at another time. The information obtained is recorded on the same chart. When this additional information has been obtained, the questioner:

- Asks for differences in actions and/or words between (or among) the instances.
- Asks for similarities among the instances.
- Asks for conclusions about people's values in this (or these) kind (or kinds) of situation(s).

Here is an example of the kind of value incident that might be used. A new student enrolls in a third-grade class in a small, rural town. His family has just moved from a larger, industrial city some three hundred miles away. After introducing the boy to the class, the teacher is called out of the classroom by the principal of the school. As soon as the teacher leaves the room, three of the other boys in the class react to the new boy. One smiles and says hello. The second asks him if he plays baseball; but when the new boy says, "No, I don't," the questioner frowns and then resumes work at his desk. The third then says in a loud voice, "Boy, what a dummy! Doesn't even play baseball."

Using the sequence suggested above, Figure 5-7 presents a series of questions and an organizational chart for student responses. It might be used to help students to make some inferences about possible values of the three boys and then to compare and contrast these inferences.

As before, question 1 asks students to identify what the different individuals in the situation said and/or did. Questions 2 and 3 ask students to make inferences as to the reasons for, and values underlying, this behavior. Question 4 asks that students try to connect the facts, reasons, and values in some way to indicate what specific sayings, actions, and/or reasons cause them to think the individuals involved value what they do. Questions 5 and 6 ask for observed differences and similarities in the behavior of the individuals in the incident. Question 7 asks for tentative conclusions that might explain why people act in certain ways in various situations.

---

1. Can we ever be certain about what a person values?

2. Value charts such as the one shown in Figure 5-6 often reveal that people are inconsistent in both words and deeds over time. Is this good or bad? How would you explain such inconsistency?

3. Some frequently cited observations are: different people value different things; the same person may value different things at different times; and the values of a person may change over time. How would you explain these observations?

Questions ↓	Boy # 1	Boy # 2	Boy # 3
1. What happened?			
2. Why did this happen?			
3. What do you think this boy values?			
4. What makes you think he values this?			
5. What differences do you notice in what the boys did?			
6. What similarities do you notice in what the boys did?			
7. Why do you think people act the way they do in these sorts of situations?			

FIGURE 5-7 Comparing and contrasting the values of different individuals in the same situation.

DESIGNING LEARNING ACTIVITIES TO PROMOTE VALUING

The nature of the subject matter which students are exposed to and asked to discuss, as well as the questions they are asked, therefore, is very important in getting them to think about values. Equally important, if not more so, to the development of values are the types of learning activities in which students are asked to participate in order to help them understand the subject matter to which they are exposed. Before I offer some suggestions about such activities, a distinction should be made between an activity and an objective. An objective is a goal to be attained, a desired outcome of instruction. An activity is any learning experience designed to help students attain a specific objective. Any one activity may serve many objectives. On the other hand, many activities may be possible (and sometimes necessary) to attain a given objective. The appropriateness of a particular activity depends on the objectives one has in mind and the degree to which the activity can help students attain that objective.

The important thing is to vary the *kinds* of activities in which students are asked to participate as much as possible in order to maintain interest and prevent boredom. The nature of any *particular* activity, however, should always depend on the nature of the particular objectives that one wishes to attain. Some key questions for teachers to ask in this regard are always, "What do I hope to accomplish?" "Why am I asking students to participate in this activity?" "What does this activity have to do with values?" "Will the activity help students understand the values of others or of themselves?"

In some cases, the objective one has in mind may be to have students acquire certain *abilities* or *behaviors,* such as being able to infer values from statements or actions, to explain something from another person's point of view, to predict consequences, to offer reasoned explanations of a value position, or to propose alternative solutions to a value dilemma. In other cases, one's objective may be to have students become able to create (or improve on) certain kinds of *products,* such as essays, charts, poems, songs, or photographs that have to do with values. And in still other cases, the objective may be primarily to engage students in a variety of values-related *experiences* (such as having them watch a film about acts of courage, role play a value incident or value dilemma, or talk with different kinds of people about values [see Figure 5-8]).

This third category, that of engaging students in a variety of different experiences, is especially important to the development of values. To gain some sense and understanding of how people feel and think, as

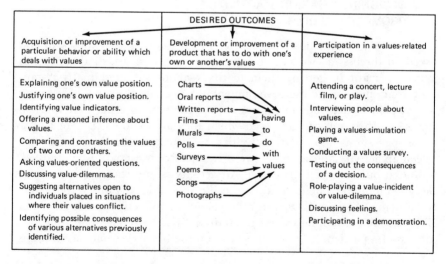

FIGURE 5-8 *Categories of learning activities designed to promote valuing.*

well as why they act and react as they do, students must be helped to "step inside their shoes" as much as possible. One's view of the world and the types of people within it is likely to be rather narrow until one has had the opportunity to experience (at the very least, vicariously) the life styles of other people—to work, play, or argue with them, participate in their sports, hear their music, see their art, discuss their politics, live as they do, and talk with them about their lives and values. Reading and hearing lectures about other people is of some help in this regard; seeing films and filmstrips about them even better; role playing better still; direct experiences such as working with others of different backgrounds and experiences on a common problem or task the best of all.

No matter what type of outcome they are after (behavior, product, or experience), learning activities can also be classified in terms of the functions they serve. For example, some provide essentially for the *intake* of information. These activities include reading, observing, interviewing, listening, or viewing (e.g., films, books, people, records, newspapers, etc.). Intake activities are essential ones for teachers to plan for, since students must have information to think about and work with before they can be expected to draw any sorts of intelligent conclusions about values, either for themselves or other people. They must have data before they can do anything with it. Raw data alone, however, are but perceptions. Perceptions must be organized and internalized if they are to be of much use. Thus the necessity for a second type of learning activity that facilitates the *organization* of information previously acquired. Examples of this type of activity include charting, note-taking, outlining, diagramming, questioning, summarizing, and sorting. These can help students organize and make sense out of the material to which they are exposed, and thus help them begin to understand the values of different people and (at least to some degree) the reasons that cause them to hold such values.

A third type of learning activity helps students to *demonstrate* what they have learned. Such activities as role playing, discussing, preparing murals, writing essays and original plays, and question formulating help students to display the skills they possess or are developing, to demonstrate how well they can analyze alternatives and consequences, and to indicate how well they understand the needs, feelings, or values of others.

A fourth type of learning activity encourages students to *express* themselves by creating or developing an original product. Expressions of this type of learning include composing a poem or song, writing a short story, illustrating a value by means of dance or drawing. Though they overlap to some degree, the essential difference between expressive and demonstrative activities is that demonstrative activities ask students to illustrate the degree to which they *understand* data they have previously acquired and organized. Expressive activities, on the other hand, encourage students to use their newly acquired understanding to produce a *new*

Intake	Organizational	Demonstrative	Expressive
Reading about	Charting	Role-playing	Composing songs about
Observing	Outlining	Discussing	Composing poems about
Interviewing	Diagramming	Explaining	Writing about
Listening to	Note-taking	Inferring	Role-playing
Touching	Asking questions about	Justifying	Miming
Surveying	Answering questions about	Indentifying	Singing
Participating in	Formulating questions about	Listing	Dancing
	Summarizing	Grouping	Drawing
Value judgments	Time-lining	Labeling	Painting
Value incidents	Drawing	Summarizing	Sketching
Value dilemmas	Cartooning	Generalizing	Cartooning
Value experiences	Sketching	Analyzing	Building
Feelings		Comparing	Imagining
	Information about values and feelings	Contrasting	Predicting
		Formulating conclusions about	Hypothesizing about
		Simulating	Proposing
		Testing	Modeling
			Simulating
		Values	Values
		Value-judgments	Value-judgments
		Value-incidents	Value-incidents
		Value-dilemmas	Value-dilemmas
		Feelings	Value-alternatives
			Consequences of
			Consequences

FIGURE 5-9 Types of learning activities categorized by function.

and different product or to render an original performance (see Figure 5-9).

Realization of the fact that different types of learning activities can serve different functions can help teachers design learning activities to think about and investigate values in a variety of ways. In too many classrooms, students are engaged in the same kind of activities, with too little variety. They listen to teachers talk; they read; they write. These kinds of activities, of course, are very important. But many students do not learn very well via talk and the printed word. They need to be more actively involved. It is for this reason that more direct activities, such as field trips, role playing, committee work, small group discussions, interviewing, asking and formulating questions to ask of speakers from different backgrounds and other cultures, composing, taking photographs, working in the community—in short, any and all activities involving doing things as well as passively receiving information—are so important for students to engage in as teachers plan for classroom (and out-of-classroom) activities to promote valuing and value inquiry. Students need to learn from books and other printed materials, to be sure, but they also need to learn from audiovisual media, from discussing, from observing, from interviewing, from taking things and ideas apart, from putting things and ideas together, from putting themselves in other people's shoes, and from feeling. When it comes to values, it is especially important for teachers to provide as many opportunities as possible for students to propose a variety of *alternatives* (for example, a variety of inferences, comparisons, ways of acting, solutions to problems, etc.) *and then to help them experience the consequences* that can result from choosing *one* of these alternatives.

If teachers are to help students learn about values (or anything else), all four categories need to be considered and planned for. They might be thought of as part of a hierarchical chain, with each type necessary to, yet building on, the others, as Figure 5-10 illustrates.

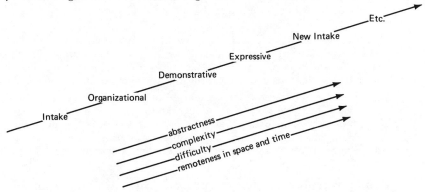

FIGURE 5-10   The chain of learning activities.

Too often, I think, we concentrate unduly on activities that provide for intake (often engaging students in two or three or even more intake activities in a row), while overlooking or minimizing organizing, demonstrating, and expressive opportunities. It is the organizing, demonstrating, and expressive types of learning activities, however, that help students to *understand* (make sense out of) data and to use what they have learned in new and different ways.

In sum, then, value activities should provide opportunities for students to:

- suggest various ways that they would *react* in situations involving another person (e.g., through discussions with other students and the teacher about ways to react; by asking continually of students "what else could be done?"; or "what else could one do?"; etc.).
- work out the possible *consequences* of an action on both themselves and other people (e.g., by discussing "what might happen?" were a particular choice to be made or event or series of events to occur; by identifying as many people as they can who might be involved in a particular situation and how they might be affected; by diagramming possible interrelationships that might exist between people involved in a value dilemma and the choices which they might make; etc.).
- identify how other people and they themselves *feel* in various situations (e.g., through discussions with the teacher and other students about feelings; by role playing people placed in difficult or unusual situations; by attempting to represent different emotional states or attitudes; etc.).
- take on the *role* of another person (e.g., by role playing various members of a family talking about their beliefs, fears, occupations, sports, etc.; by role playing both [or several] sides of an argument; by discussing how one feels in a dyadic conflict situation; by describing or discussing what one would do in such situations; etc.).
- *identify alternative* courses of action that might be pursued in various situations (e.g., by listing various options that a person faced with a value choice might consider; by role playing different ways of resolving a problem; by being presented with and asked to choose from among a number of options; etc.).
- *evaluate* various *alternatives* from several points of view (e.g., by discussing various [legal, economic, aesthetic, prudential, moral, health, etc.] effects of a given action; by charting or diagramming such effects; by debating the pros and cons of suggested proposals; etc.).
- *assess* predicted *consequences* of proposed alternative policies or actions in terms of both the likelihood and desirability of their occurrence (e.g., by ranking consequences in terms of these two criteria; by preparing charts in this regard; by comparing and contrasting consequences in terms not only of their short-range, but also their long-range effects; etc.).

In short, therefore, it is important for teachers to think about not only *what* they want students to learn, but also *how* they expect them to learn it. Knowledge alone will not encourage students to think about or develop values; will not change attitudes; will not build value-analysis skills. These goals are achieved primarily by having students *use* the knowledge that they acquire. On the other hand, students cannot improve their reasoning about value issues, clarify their feelings, or improve their skills unless they are provided with some data to think about and use. One cannot in reality separate subject matter and learning activities, for they go hand in hand. Both must be considered and planned for by teachers who wish to help students explore and think about values in their classrooms.

---

1. Look at the categories of learning activities in Figure 5-8. What additional outcomes (if any) besides behaviors, products, or experiences might a teacher interested in developing values want to help students attain?

2. Look at functional categorization of learning activities in Figure 5-9. What other activities would you suggest in each category? What other categories (that is, other than intake, organizational, demonstrative, expressive), if any, would you suggest?

EXPLORING FEELINGS

As mentioned in Chapter 1, values are not only ideas; they are also emotional commitments. They contain a very strong "feelings" component. People have very strong feelings about the things they value.

Earlier in this chapter we considered some strategies designed to help students identify, compare, and contrast people's values. Many values that students will identify, however, will be different than their own. Therefore, if students are to be helped not only to identify others' values but also to *understand why* they are different values than their own, teachers will need to increase student sensitivity of how others *feel* in a variety of situations. How can this be done?

To increase student sensitivity to the feelings of others, they should be provided with opportunities to talk about feelings, to identify with the feelings of other people, and to react emotionally themselves. Teachers, then, should encourage and help students to participate in experiences that allow them to feel many different kinds of emotions, to come into contact with many different people (directly or vicariously), to do different things, and then to share their perceptions of and feelings about these experiences. The *particular* experiences in which students are to be engaged should always depend on their levels of sophistication and the teacher's analysis of the type of experience appropriate to their needs and abilities. Some examples of the kinds of experiences I have in mind follow.

1. Visit a home for the aged.
2. Take a walk on a littered beach.
3. Give someone a flower every day for a week.
4. Spend a day in a wheelchair or on crutches.
5. Conduct a door-to-door survey of a random number of homes in your neighborhood as to what the occupants feel is wrong (or right) with your community.
6. Work in a political campaign.
7. Compare prices for the same food items at different stores.
8. Listen to a tape recording of Dr. Martin Luther King, Jr.'s speech, "I Have a Dream."
9. Try to go without food for a whole day.
10. Talk to a blind person about what it's like to be blind.
11. Spend a day with a police officer.
12. Observe a bargain sale at a downtown department store.
13. Take a young child to the zoo.
14. Smile at everyone you meet for a week.
15. Try not to talk for a whole day.
16. Ask a rehabilitated alcoholic to speak to the class about why he or she drank.
17. Volunteer some time to help patients in a hospital for the mentally ill.
18. Negotiate a student bill of rights with the principal of your school.
19. Talk with some elderly people every day for a week.
20. Take your Mom (or Dad) for a walk.
21. Interview members of the A.S.P.C.A. as to how many unwanted animals they must dispose of a year and how they do it.
22. Listen to Isaac Stern play the violin.
23. Write a poem about love.

After students have participated in experiences similar to those above they should be encouraged (not required, of course) to talk about how they felt and why. This can help them to realize the differences in values and feelings that people have. A helpful rule of thumb here is to proceed as follows:

- Ask for facts.
- Ask for inferences about reasons.
- Ask for inferences about feelings.
- Check for similar or different feelings.
- Ask for conclusions.

Here is an example of a set of questions organized to do this:

1. What did you do? (Where did you go, what happened to you, and so on?)

2. How did you feel?
3. Anybody else feel this way?
4. After listening to the experiences that people have had, what can you say about people and how they feel in situations like this?

Question 1 asks students to describe the situation in which they were involved and what they did. Question 2 asks them to relate their feelings —their emotional *reactions* to what they experienced. Question 3 allows students (we hope) to realize that many people may feel things quite differently but also that many frequently *feel quite similarly to the way they do.* Question 4 then asks students to draw conclusions about people's feelings.

The assumption underlying these activities and questions is that by forming and comparing inferences about their own and others' feelings, students will become more aware of the *similarities* between people's feelings in various situations. Students thus will be better able to understand how and why people feel and act as they do.

Role Playing

Another way to help students explore feelings is to engage them in role playing. Role playing requires students to act out the roles of imaginary or real people in various situations where their feelings and values come into play. Value incidents and value dilemmas provide many possibilities for role playing. Consider, for example, any of the value incidents on pages 94, 95, or 96 or the value dilemmas on pages 65, 68, or 127. Role playing is particularly useful in helping students to become aware of how people who are deprived, discriminated against, abused, or oppressed feel. Consider these examples:

- You are the owner of a small shop in a very poor neighborhood. You have just caught a ten-year-old boy attempting to steal some candy from your store. You know his mother is on welfare. What do you do?
- You live in a small community that recently has been ordered to integrate its schools. You are strongly opposed to the use of busing as a way to accomplish such integration. A number of your friends inform you that they plan to harass a busload of elementary school children on their way to school tomorrow to protest busing. They indicate they expect you to join them. What do you do?
- You are an American pilot in Vietnam. Your squadron has just received orders to bomb an area five miles in diameter the next day in order to support an infantry attack. You know that there are three villages in this area in which hundreds of Vietnamese civilians live. What do you do?
- You are a prison guard in a state penitentiary. The prisoners in solitary confinement are not allowed to have books or magazines in their cells or

to talk to anyone during their period of punishment. One prisoner with whom you previously have been friendly asks you to give him a book secretly. What do you do?

• You are a reporter on a large city newspaper. You have just discovered that your closest and most trusted friend owns a run-down hotel in the worst area of the city and that he charges the pensioners and elderly people who live there exorbitant rates. What do you do?

The Shaftels suggest that role playing involves the following steps: [7]

1. Warm-up (teacher introduction and presentation of the dilemmas to be acted out). The dilemma—in printed, visual, oral, or audio form—is presented to the class up to the moment that a decision must be made. The teacher (or questioner) then asks the class: "What do you think (the key character) should (or might) do?"

2. Selecting the role players (choosing the students to portray the various roles in the dilemma). Students who have identified with characters in the dilemmas should be encouraged to assume their roles. If necessary, volunteers should be requested to play them. The Shaftels suggests students who have been *volunteered* for roles by others should not be assigned such roles, since the reasons behind this may be punitive. In addition, the suggested student may not see himself or herself in such a role. [8]

3. Preparing the rest of the class to be observed. To help other students zero in on the role playing, they can be assigned to different observer tasks. They can be asked to judge how realistic the role playing is and especially to think about how the characters depicted feel as the role playing progresses.

4. Setting the stage. This involves giving the role players some time to plan briefly what they will do and how they will do it. The teacher also should check to be sure that the necessary materials or props (usually very simple ones such as a desk, chair, a few scattered objects) are available.

5. The enactment. Students act out the roles they have chosen. Shaftel points out that role players should be reminded that they are not being condemned or praised for their portrayals. Students are not being evaluated on their acting ability. [9] The central purpose of role playing is to help students gain some insights into the feelings and values of other people.

6. Discussion and evaluation. This is a sort of debriefing stage where teacher and class discuss what happened, how realistic the role playing was, and how likely it is that the consequences as depicted actually would occur.

[7] Fannie R. Shaftel and George Shaftel, *Role-Playing for Social Values: Decision-Making in the Social Studies* (Englewood Cliffs, N.J.: Prentice-Hall, 1967), p. 84.
[8] Ibid., p. 76.
[9] Ibid., p. 79.

7. Further enactments. This stage provides an opportunity for the role players to reenact the dilemma or for it to be replayed with different students in the roles.

8. Further discussion. Once again, the role playing should be debriefed, with the class discussing the new enactment, changes made in the outcome of the dilemma, how realistic it was, and so on.

9. Generalizing. At this point, the teacher asks the class to draw some conclusions about what they observed and felt and then to discuss their conclusions. Some sort of wrap-up question such as, "Why do you think people placed in situations like this act the way they do?" or, "How do people in these sorts of situations feel and why?" can be quite helpful.

A word of caution at this point. It is important that a teacher not indicate approval or disapproval of those feelings that he personally endorses or does not endorse. A student's reactions concerning her experiences in the world are uniquely personal and private and should be respected as such, provided they are not imposed on others.

Even though we may disapprove of a student's feelings, we must accept the student as a person of sensitivity and worth if we are to help her to understand and accept the fact that different kinds of feelings can be experienced in the same or similar situations. This can be done in a number of ways. A teacher can listen carefully and respond in a non-judgmental manner (e.g., by nodding or saying, "I see"). He can restate what a student has said while indicating that he understands what the student is trying to express. (For example, "You said you felt very uncomfortable when you moved to a new town and began your freshman year in high school away from all your old friends. I can understand that kind of feeling.") He can support the feelings a student expresses ("I know what you mean, Paula; I've felt that way myself").

Sometimes teachers and other adults do attempt to dictate to students how they should feel or react to a particular experience, as the following dialogue illustrates:

T: Now I want you to listen to some Stravinsky. You'll find this is much more beautiful than Sibelius. (Teacher plays "Rite of Spring.")

T: As you heard, Stravinsky is much more intense—he gives you more feeling.

S: I got more feeling from Sibelius.

T: From Sibelius?

S: Yeah, I like him better. He makes me feel excited inside.

T: Well, that doesn't make sense. His music isn't as vibrant, or challenging.

S: Well, I still like Sibelius. In fact, I don't like Stravinsky at all.

T: Well, that's not true. And George, when I ask you which music is more vibrant on the exam, the correct answer will be Stravinsky.[10]

This may be a somewhat exaggerated example, but it does point up what might happen if teachers are not careful. The point being stressed here is that when it comes to feelings, the teacher must try not to judge. What they should try to do, however, is to engage students in a rich variety of experiences so that they continually expand their awareness and understanding of the feelings of other people.

---

1. Are there any kinds of feelings teachers should not explore with students? Why? Should the students' feelings be discussed by a teacher in class? Why or why not?

2. Should students be encouraged to discuss how teachers might feel in various situations? Why or why not?

3. Many people feel uncomfortable when asked to talk about their feelings. How would you explain this?

4. Should a teacher ever indicate approval or disapproval of a student's feelings? Why or why not? What if those feelings are antidemocratic or prejudiced in nature?

EXERCISES

1. Here are some statements of rationale that have been proposed for teaching values in the schools. How many, if any, do you think are justifiable? What others would you add?

   a. So that students will learn what is right and proper.
   b. Because there is no way to avoid doing so anyway.
   c. Because it will help them clarify what their own values are.
   d. Because it will help them to understand other people more fully.
   e. Because teachers have a professional responsibility to do so.
   f. In order to help students realize that honest men and women may legitimately differ in their views as to what is important in life.

2. In which category from Column A (Fact, Definition, or Inference) would you place each of the questions in Column B? Why?

Column A	Column B
Questions	___ 1. Why do you think that occurred?
that Ask for	___ 2. Can you give me an example of a "chauvinist"?
Facts (F)	___ 3. What would you say Timothy considers important?

[10] David J. Bond, "The Fact-Value Myth," *Social Education*, February 1970, pp. 186–190.

Questions that Ask for Definitions (D)	___ 4. What happened in this instance?
	___ 5. What might have happened to the civil rights movement if Martin Luther King had not been assassinated?
Questions that Ask for Inferences (I)	___ 6. When was the Magna Charta signed?
	___ 7. What do you mean by "valuable"?
	___ 8. How has life in the United States since 1945 differed from life before World War II?
	___ 9. Why did Mrs. Adams consider that a threatening remark?

3. Here is an excerpt from a hypothetical text on American government similar to those used in many schools throughout the United States:

> Early in 1972, Congress sent to the fifty States the proposed 27th Amendment—the "women's rights amendment"—for ratification. This amendment prohibits discrimination by the Federal Government and the States on account of sex. Although the amendment passed the House with only sixteen dissenting votes, and eighty-three Senators were co-sponsors of the amendment, there were opponents to the amendment who argued that it was an unnecessary law. They argued that abolition of the laws which discriminate against women can best be brought about by testing them in the courts on a case-by-case basis.

Write a question in each of the categories below, directing such questions specifically to the above passage:

A question asking for a *fact:* _____

_____

A question asking for a *definition:* _____

_____

A question asking for an *inference about reasons:* _____

_____

A question asking for an *inference about values:* _____

_____

4. It is helpful to think about the *order* or *sequence* in asking questions. One suggestion is that factual-type questions should precede inferential-type questions and that definitional-type questions should be asked whenever the need arises (i.e., whenever the meaning of a term is

so unclear that it impedes discussion). For any sort of questioning sequence to make sense, the questions involved must be asked with a definite purpose in mind. Given the sequence suggested above, how would you arrange the questions below? Why? (Students previously have been asked to read two accounts of slave life during the 1850s, one about life on a plantation in Mississippi, one about life on a plantation in Alabama.)

——In what ways were the lives of Jenny and Millie different?
——Why was Millie treated as she was?
——Under what kind of conditions did Jenny live?
——How would you explain these similarities?
——How were Millie and Jenny's lives similar?
——Under what kind of conditions did Millie live?
——Why was Jenny treated as she was?
——How would you explain these differences?

5. Try out some of the procedures described in this chapter. What difficulties do you encounter? Would you change the steps involved in any way? If so, how?

6. Try out some of the strategies described in this chapter with both elementary and secondary students. What difficulties do you encounter? Would you change the steps involved in the strategies in any way? If so, how?

7. Role play some of the value dilemmas and/or value incidents in this book (see pages 57, 61, and 109), using the steps described on pages 110–11. Would you change the order of these steps in any way? If so, how? Would you recommend adding any steps? Why or why not?

8. How effective, as compared with films, stories, and so on, would you judge role playing as a way of *presenting* students with value incidents? Which way would you say is most effective—visually (films and filmstrips); orally (stories presented on tape, record, or by voice); or in writing (being asked to read the value incident)? Why?

9. Here are a number of activities that different people have suggested could be used to engage students in valuing. Into which category (intake, organizational, demonstrative, or expressive) would you place each? Why?

- composing a song about one's feelings
- role playing a value incident
- playing a values-simulation game
- surveying a sample of one's community concerning what they like or dislike about politicians
- reading John F. Kennedy's *Profiles in Courage*

- outlining a person's position as expressed in a speech on "morality in government"
- attending an avant garde film
- discussing the values of individuals as portrayed in various television programs
- preparing a list of questions to ask a guest speaker in order to gain some idea of what the speaker considers important

10. Look at each of the activities presented in Figure 5-8. Into what category (intake, organizational, demonstrative, or expressive) would you place each? Why?

chapter six

ANALYZING VALUES

We saw in Chapter 2 that some of the statements people make can provide clues about what they value. Statements that suggest what people like, what something is worth, or what should be done are called value judgments. Students regularly come across such judgments, both in and out of the classroom. Thus, helping them to analyze and assess such statements can only be to their benefit. Since value judgments are made for a reason, learning to seek out and assess these reasons can help students decide if particular judgments are ones they would make themselves.

ANALYZING VALUE JUDGMENTS

As mentioned earlier, value judgments can appear in a variety of forms. Some may be indications of personal taste (e.g., "I like to listen to the symphony very much"). This type of value judgment can be checked out by a little routine detective work. We need to observe the speaker or obtain some reliable reports of his or her behavior over time. Does this person actually go to the symphony? Are there reports of his or her attendance at symphony concerts? Does he or she listen to the symphony on the radio or television when possible?

Some value judgments are assertions that a particular object or class of objects will bring a certain price in the marketplace (e.g., "That painting is worth $1,500 in hard cash from any reputable art dealer in the country"). This type of judgment can be verified easily by visiting (or even phoning) a reputable, professional art dealer. As mentioned earlier, both these two types of value judgments are really factual judgments in disguise.

Other value judgments are more generalized assertions about the quality or worth of something (e.g., "Eleanor Roosevelt was a great person"). We might call this type *definitional* value judgments. Still others indicate that some person or group should do a particular thing or follow a particular course of action (e.g., "The United States should cease giving any aid whatsoever to dictatorships"). We might call this type *propositional* value judgments. Most disagreements over values revolve around one of *these* two types of value judgments. How can we help students to analyze each? [1]

If individuals are to assess definitional value claims intelligently, they first must be clear about what the claim means. For example, if someone remarks that Joanna is an excellent worker, we need to know what is meant by the term *excellent* (that is, what qualities, skills, and so on, an excellent worker possesses) before we can assess Joanna's work. How can we tell an excellent worker from one who is only so-so? What characteristics does an excellent worker possess that a poor or mediocre worker lacks? The teacher's task here is to help students define the term and then to ask the class to consider whether the individual involved (Joanna) fits the definition—i.e., possesses the characteristics.

Many value disputes arise because people have different meanings in mind for the value terms they use. For example, suppose a student states that Eleanor Roosevelt was a great person. If the class is to discuss and assess this value judgment, the term *great* must be defined. What characteristics do great men and women possess? The teacher's job is to encourage and help students to define the value term and then to help them to decide whether a particular person in a given situation (in this case, Eleanor Roosevelt) would fall within the definition—that is, would possess the characteristics.

The problem here, as you can guess, lies in reaching an agreement on the definition of *great*. Such a word, since it is an abstraction, is very difficult to pin down to a precise meaning. However, the teacher must encourage and help students to make the attempt so that the meaning of various alternatives becomes clearer.

A student might define such a term as *great* in different ways. She might translate it into terms more easily understood (for instance, *great* means "famous," "renowned the world over"). She might point to an example or examples of several persons and/or their actions that she considers great, indicating the characteristics or attributes they possess that make them great.

1 Part of what follows in this section has been adapted from Jack R. Fraenkel, "Strategies For Developing Values," *Today's Education*, November-December 1973, pp. 49–55.

Here is an illustration of a teacher asking a student for an example to clarify the meaning of a term:

S: Malcolm X was a pretty cool dude.

T: What do you mean by "cool?"

S: You know, bad!

T: Hmm. Could you give us an example to illustrate what you mean? What kinds of things did Malcolm X do that make you think he was cool or bad?

S: Well, he kind of thought out how people have to live in order to keep their self-respect. And he tried to live that way, too.

T: And what way was that?

S: Not to do something if it put you down . . .

The more characteristics the student can identify, the better, since it then becomes easier to determine the degree to which a given individual deserves the label in question. Thus, greatness might be attributed to a person who (a) holds a high (a term that also would have to be defined) office, (b) is recognized for high achievement in his or her field, (c) has contributed to the betterment of mankind. According to this definition, a person would have to meet all three criteria to be considered great.

Newmann has suggested three attributes that can be used as guidelines in determining if a particular definition is adequate.[2]

1) It should be noncircular; that is, it should not contain language that is the same or only slightly different from the term being defined (e.g., defining a democracy as a "country with a democratic government").

2) It should be convertible; that is, the term to be defined should "equal" the definition (e.g., the definition of a slave as "a human being who is the legal property of another" is equally true when reversed).

3) It should be sufficiently precise to distinguish among examples that differ in subtle ways.

However, when a student defines a term, it is quite possible that other students will disagree with the definition. When that happens, the teacher has two possible alternatives. One possibility is to ask the class to consult a dictionary. A second is for the participants to agree among themselves that the term means such-and-such in *this* instance (though not necessarily beyond this instance) so that discussion may proceed. If students are unable to agree on a stipulation, the class will have no recourse but to "agree to disagree" for the time being and to continue the search for meanings upon which they can concur.

[2] Fred M. Newmann with Donald W. Oliver, *Clarifying Public Controversy: An Approach to Teaching Social Studies* (Boston: Little, Brown, 1970), pp. 53–54.

If students are to assess propositional value judgments intelligently, they must not only be clear about the value terms involved. They also must consider what might happen if the proposition were to become reality. Suppose, for example, that during a class discussion on international politics, a student claims that the possession of armaments by nation-states should be limited to small-scale weapons. Other students disagree, arguing that those nations capable of manufacturing and/or otherwise obtaining heavier armaments are entitled to build as large and powerful a store of armaments as they wish. Helping students to understand the specifics of the claims and to come to some defensible conclusions of their own requires that a teacher engage them in several operations. The value term or terms must be defined, and the consequences that might result from both proposals must be identified and evaluated.

First, the problem of defining the value term. There are two things the teacher might do. He or she can ask for examples of what the student means by a "small-scale" weapon. It often is helpful for the teacher to suggest examples to help the student clarify what he means for himself and for the class. Does the term include anything larger than a machine gun? What about such weapons-carrying vehicles as tanks? How about submarines? Aircraft carriers? Bombers? Hand grenades? Small-scale nuclear rockets? Or, the teacher also can ask students for the defining characteristics of a small-scale weapon (can any weapon that drops bombs be considered "small-scale?").

When the meaning of the value term is clear (at least for the purposes of the discussion at hand), consequences must be investigated. What is likely to happen if such a policy as the one being advocated is followed? Are there any examples of nations disarming to this extent in the past? If so, what happened to them? These are factual-type questions, and they require students to do some research to see what they can find out. Historical records, documents, photographs, eyewitness accounts, newspaper reports, diaries, journals—all are grist for the mill. As much relevant and documented information as possible should be collected.

All data offered as evidence to support or refute the likelihood that a consequence will occur then must be checked for relevance and accuracy. We determine the relevance of data by checking to see if they refer to the particular consequence being considered. We check the accuracy of data by determining if what are presented or referred to is correct—i.e., are not in error, fake, or revised in some way.

When students are unable to find historical parallels the teacher must encourage the class to *think out* what *might* happen. In our previous example, will the countries who disarm benefit in some way? If so, how? What about those countries that don't disarm—won't they be able and likely to take advantage of the others? Who would see to it that such disarmament actually takes place? What kinds of expenses would be involved? What might be the repercussions of such disarmament on people in the future?

Students most likely will predict consequences depending on their previous inclination toward the policy being advocated. Those in favor of disarming will predict favorable consequences; those against disarming will predict unfavorable consequences. Usually, however, they are unaware of some possible consequences; and it is the teacher's responsibility to present additional examples that illustrate the consequences of following a given policy.

Notice that obtaining as much relevant and documented information as possible is extremely important. Students cannot make intelligent productions about consequences if they have no data with which to work or if they have no idea how to use the data they do collect.

---

1. "The more characteristics the student can identify, the better, since it then becomes easier to determine the degree to which a given individual deserves the label in question." It also becomes progressively more difficult to find such individuals. At what point would you say the identification of characteristics should cease?

2. Can you suggest any other ways in which value judgments might be analyzed and assessed besides those presented here? If so, what are they?

3. Should a teacher ever discuss value judgments that are indications of personal taste? Why or why not? What about value judgments that students make about other students? About teachers?

4. Are there any kinds of value judgments that you think teachers should *not* analyze with students? If so, why not?

SOME COMMENTS ABOUT EVIDENCE

A student can present a number of different kinds of evidence to support or refute his or her assertion that a particular consequence or set of consequences will occur. Such evidence includes personal belief, authoritative opinion, logical reasoning, personal observation, or documentation.[3]

Personal belief. One kind of evidence that a student might offer in support of a predicted consequence is the personal belief that it is so. Evidence to support his claim is his own personal, unique, and subjective opinion. When pressed to support this personal belief (that is, when asked, "Why do you believe this?" or "Why do you think that is so?") the student may fall back on *intuition.* That is, he may state that he intuitively "knows" or "feels" that what he is claiming is so. Here is an example:

Phil: Lots of countries would support limiting arms to the small-scale level.

T: Why do you think they would be willing to do this? (Request for evidence.)

Phil: I just have a hunch that they would.

Phil's evidence in this instance is his own opinion or "feeling." He has a "hunch" that something would happen. The major difficulty with this kind of evidence, however, is that it is essentially private in nature. Phil is not providing his classmates or the teacher with any data that they can evaluate to see if such data logically or empirically support the likelihood of the consequence occurring. Corroboration of the suggested consequence is being argued on private (i.e., nonverifiable) rather than public grounds.

Notice that getting students to offer their opinions in the classroom is to be desired—in fact, it is essential if value discussions are to take place. But offering an opinion that is to be investigated and subsequently

---

[3] See Donald W. Oliver and James P. Shaver, *Teaching Public Issues in the High School* (Boston: Houghton-Mifflin, 1966), for an excellent treatment of the importance of evidence.

supported or refuted on the basis of evidence is not the same thing as offering an opinion *as* evidence itself.

Authoritative opinion. A second kind of evidence a student might offer to support a claim is the consensus or agreement of others. Much of the strength of this kind of evidence, of course, depends on who the "others" are.

Suppose, for example, that Phil supports his statement that "lots of countries would support limiting arms to the small-scale level" by offering the following evidence: a consensus of opinion among several noted political scientists and other observers who specialize in the study of international affairs and are considered authorities or "experts" in the field. This might be accepted by many students as considerable evidence to support Phil's statement.

A question remains, however, as to the degree to which one is willing to accept, or is justified in accepting, the views of experts. Whenever the viewpoint of an authority is cited as evidence by a student to support a claim, the rest of the class is faced with the question of the authority's *reliability.* Ennis suggests using the following criteria to test the value of an authority's opinion.

1. He has a good reputation.
2. The statement (claim) is in his field.
3. He was disinterested.
4. His reputation could be affected by his statement, and he was aware of this fact when he made his statement.
5. He studied the matter covered by the statement (i.e., the student's claim).
6. He followed accepted procedures in coming to decide that he was entitled to make his statement.
7. He was in full possession of his faculties.
8. He is not in disagreement with others who meet the above criteria for authorities.[4]

Ennis points out that the joint satisfaction of all these criteria makes a very strong case for considering the view(s) of an authority reliable in a particular instance.

The danger with authoritative evidence, however, lies in the fact that authorities can make mistakes, too. In Galileo's day, for example, the authorities of the time were convinced that the earth was the center of the universe. During the Middle Ages, medical authorities believed that bleeding patients was a cure for fever. Just because an expert "knows" more than a layman does not make him infallible.

4 Robert H. Ennis, *Logic in Teaching* (Englewood Cliffs, N.J.: Prentice-Hall, 1969), p. 393.

Personal observation, documentation, or experimentation. A third type of evidence a student might offer to support a claim is that she personally has observed or performed whatever she is referring to. This kind of evidence has its limitations, too, however. The student then must prove that she has observed accurately. The factor of personal bias may be involved, since people often are influenced by prejudices of which they are unaware. Whenever possible, therefore, students should be encouraged to find and present photographs, pictures, records, or tapes that show that an event has occurred. This type of evidence is difficult to obtain on any kind of regular basis, but there are occasions when an audio or visual reproduction of an event is available. This is particularly true with regard to pictures from newspapers and magazines. Hence, it is helpful for a teacher to insure that the class subscribes to a variety of newspapers and newsmagazines encompassing a fairly wide spectrum of political and other opinion.

Some claims lend themselves to experimentation—that is, the student actually can try things out to see what happens. Consider the example that follows.

Al: You can find out more about how people feel about disarming by reading the newspaper over a period of time than you can by reading articles written by political scientists.

Susan: No, you can't.

T: Well, why don't you two check this out? Do some research in the public library. Look at what the newspapers had to say when the disarmament talks were in full swing last year. Then gather together some recent articles by some political scientists and other commentators on disarmament. See which provides you with the most information about how people feel about the issue.

Logical reasoning. A fourth type of evidence a student might offer to support a factual claim is to show that the claim results from a logically valid piece of deductive reasoning. In short—the claim follows logically from certain premises as in the well-known example:

a. All men are mortal.
b. Socrates is a man.
c. Therefore, Socrates is mortal.

These three statements represent what commonly is known as a *syllogism.* The first statement is called the *major premise.* The second statement is called the *minor premise,* and the third is the *conclusion.* A set of one or more premises together with a conclusion that necessarily follows from the premises is called a *valid argument*. An invalid argument is one in which the conclusion does *not necessarily* follow from the premises. Two questions to be asked of all syllogisms are whether or not the conclusion logically follows from the premises and whether or not the conclusion is valid. In the example above, the conclusion is true because both premises are true. Whenever the major and minor premises are both true the conclusion *must* be true.

Let us consider a second example, however:

   a. Only the leaders of small, non-industrialized nations are in favor of having all the nations of the world disarm to the level of small-scale weapons.

   b. John Boorman is a leader of a small, non-industrialized nation.

   c. Therefore, Boorman is in favor of having all of the nations of the world disarm to this level.

In this case, the conclusion may be false. But why? Nothing seems wrong with the *reasoning* involved here. The reasoning *is* correct, but the conclusion arrived at *may* be false—because the major premise is false. There are some leaders in large, industrialized nations who favor disarmament to this level and also some leaders in small, non-industrialized nations who do not.

Notice that both the major and minor premises are factual assertions. Their truth or falsehood can be determined by obtaining proof of some sort (e.g., by consulting over a period of time newspapers, press releases, position papers, public interviews, and so on). When a student offers a deductive argument as evidence, therefore, one task of the teacher is to help students to determine whether the premises of the argument are true or false—that is, whether or not some proof of their existence or occurrence can be found.

It is important for teachers to help students to distinguish between valid reasoning and truth. It is common practice in a discussion for one person to try to convince others to accept a point of view by presenting a valid line of reasoning that is based on one or more false premises. The conclusion that follows may then be *logically* valid, but *factually* false. If either of the premises in a deductive argument is false the conclusion *may* be false, though not necessarily so.

One final note of caution regarding syllogistic arguments—an argument may be valid and the conclusion or conclusions stemming from it true, even if *both* premises are false. Here is an example:

   a. Coffee pots are automobiles.

   b. Automobiles are filled with coffee.

   c. Therefore, coffee pots are filled with coffee.

The argument is valid and the conclusion true, even though both premises are false, since the conclusion logically follows from the premises.

The lesson to be learned from the above example is a simple one. The fact that one or more premises of an argument is false does not necessarily mean that the conclusion that follows is false. Nor does the fact that an argument is valid necessarily mean that the conclusion is true. Only when both premises are true and the argument is valid *must* a conclusion be true (see Figure 6-1).

Just because an argument is valid does not mean that its conclusion is true. Teachers should always have students determine whether proof of the truth or of the falsehood of the premises exists.

Verifying Evidence

When a student has presented evidence (no matter what kind it is) the matter of *verification* arises. Does the evidence presented provide support (to the class's satisfaction) for the likelihood of the consequence occurring? If the evidence offered is only personal or group belief the claim cannot be verified; it must remain purely an indication of personal or group preference. If the evidence is authoritative judgment the authority's reliability must be determined, and his or her arguments must be either logically or empirically supported or refuted. If the evidence consists of a conclusion based on logical reasoning, we must check to see if the argument is valid and the premises true. If the supporting evidence consists of certain actions or certain accomplishments we must check to see whether the alleged actions indeed were performed or the accomplishments indeed achieved in similar situations.

Before any profitable discussion of various claims can take place, however, students must realize that accepting different kinds of evidence may result in quite different assessments. They must realize that different

Major premise	Minor premise	Conclusion
True	True	Must be true
True	False	Can be either true or false
False	True	" "
False	False	" "

FIGURE 6-1 Combinations of valid arguments.

people may come to quite different decisions depending on the kinds of evidence they accept. Thus, it is important for teachers to help students realize that there are different kinds of evidence that can be used to support or refute an argument. They must help them to understand that different people, depending on their background and experience, consider certain kinds of evidence more acceptable than other kinds. Students should consider what kind is most convincing with regard to a particular proposition and why. Whether a given statement is "true" or "good" can be determined only by knowing what evidence those who make the statement will accept in its support. Agreement during a values investigation and discussion is likely to be difficult to obtain, however, unless the same evidence is used.

---

1. What other kinds of evidence might be offered to support or refute the likelihood of a consequence occurring?

2. The offering of statements by students in class without evidence to back them up (or indeed by people in general) is a rather common-place occurrence. How would you explain this?

3. Which type of evidence described above would you consider the most convincing in support of an argument? Why?

4. "Agreement during a values discussion is likely to be difficult to obtain unless the same evidence is used." What does this mean? Why would this be so? What might happen if agreement is *not* obtained? Would this be good or bad?

ANALYZING VALUE CONFLICT

As mentioned in Chapter 1, individuals often are placed in situations where their values conflict. The example of the secretary who was faced with a conflict between being loyal and being honest is a case in point. Many other examples could be given. Should one be loyal to one friend if this means being disloyal to another? Should one always be honest, even if this means hurting another person's feelings? Should a teacher allow a student to speak his mind on topics that other students find offensive? Should a soldier disobey an order he thinks is immoral? Should the police use "third-degree" methods to obtain a confession from a murder suspect? Should a President order the wiretapping of telephones in the interests of "national security"? Should the United States provide aid to poor nations that are governed by dictators?

Value conflict is a fact of life. It is realistic for teachers to recognize this fact and to help students recognize it. A realization that values often conflict may help students to understand why people often are inconsistent in their behavior. How can teachers do this? How can they help students to realize that individuals often are torn by conflicting values?

One way to proceed is to present students with a *value dilemma*—a historical or contemporary situation, argument, or illustration in which an individual (or group of individuals) is faced with a *choice* between two or more conflicting yet desirable alternatives. Students can then be encouraged to discuss various actions that might be taken, along with a consideration of the possible short- and long-term consequences of these actions. This is intended to open students' eyes to the fact that often there are several possible ways of resolving a problem and that the consideration of different alternatives frequently brings to light possibilities that were not at first apparent.

Several examples of value dilemmas were presented in Chapter 4, together with a teaching strategy to engage students in a discussion of such dilemmas (see pages 61–71). The questions the developers of this strategy propose, however, focus primarily on analyzing alternative courses of action. Serious and sustained exploration of the consequences of these alternatives is not a basic part of the strategy. In the remainder of this section, therefore, I will propose a strategy that concentrates more on analyzing the consequences of alternatives.

Below is a fictionalized version of an incident that occurred on the east coast of the United States a few years back. A set of guidelines for encouraging students to consider not only alternatives but also consequences appears after the story (a value dilemma).

Tom Cosby's Dilemma [5]

Tom Cosby arrived a few minutes early at the meeting. "Far out, far out," he thought. "Who would have thought that this many people would turn out for a Board of Education meeting? Well, here goes." He hurried down the aisle to his seat on the stage. Already present, he noted, were the principal, the president of the school board, Mr. Johnson, his social studies teacher; and a couple of other people he didn't know. He also recognized many of the people in the front rows of the auditorium. His mom and dad were sitting next to the Reverend Sooners of Glide Episcopal. Mrs. Leibowitz, president of the Board of Supervisors, was there. Several union officials had shown up, along with the heads of the two Teachers' Associations. Many members of the black community could be seen, and there was a pretty good sprinkling of other minority groups as well. There was Mr. Adams of the American Civil Liberties Union, too. He remembered Adams especially, since he had liked what he had to say when he was a guest speaker in

[5] My thanks to Peg Carter of Ann Arbor, Michigan, for writing the first draft of this story.

Civics I. "Outta sight!" he almost said aloud, "Old Man Tabbett, the editor of the *Daily Express,* is here!"

Every year since 1945, the Plainsville Exchange Club had sponsored a visiting student from another country as part of an on-going student exchange program. Tom, in fact, had hoped that he might be the student chosen from Plainsville to spend the next school year —his senior year—in another country. Last year he had gotten to be pretty good friends with Alex Tomlinson, who had come to Plainsville from England. That guy could sure kick a soccer ball, all right. He'd learned a lot from Alex, he thought. But this year— this year, things were different. This year the guest student was to be a white guy named Arthur Smith from a place called Windhoek in Namibia. Tom hadn't even known such a place existed. He was pretty shook when he found out where Namibia was—in southwest Africa! He and several of the brothers in the Black Students Association were among the student leaders who had protested to the principal.

When he told his dad about it, the old man was just as angry as he was. He'd called several members of the black community, along with some other friends, that very night. Tom could still see the article that appeared in the paper a few days later.

Protest Develops over Enrollment of Exchange Student in Plainsville High

September 21—Spurred on by protesting students at Plainsville High School, many members of the local community today picketed in front of the Board of Education to protest the forthcoming arrival and enrollment of Arthur Smith, an exchange student from Windhoek, Namibia, a territory illegally controlled by South Africa. Young Smith's invitation was part of the Student Exchange Program sponsored by the local Cultural Exchange Club.

Protesters complained of the expressed governmental policy in South Africa of complete racial segregation of whites, blacks, and Asians, and requested that Smith's invitation be rescinded and that another student, from a country which does not endorse segregation, be invited in his place. Neither the head of the Cultural Exchange Club nor the President of the Board of Education was available for comment on the matter.

Things really began to hit the fan then! The NAACP got into the act and publically denounced the invitation at the next meeting of the school board. The commander of the American Legion Post sent a strong letter to the editor of the paper protesting Smith's enrollment.

What had surprised Tom, however, had been the response of Old Man Tabbett, the editor of the paper. He had not agreed with the protesters. Some of the words of Tabbett's editorial of last week still stuck in Tom's mind.

. . . this is not an issue of government policy. Arthur Smith did not formulate and cannot be held responsible for the actions of his government. He may not be aware of all that such a policy implies. One thing, however, is certain. Arthur Smith will be unlikely to consider alternatives to such a policy unless he has the opportunity to experience other ways of dealing with people. How, we might ask, is he to obtain such experience if he is denied the opportunity to meet and interact with others who perhaps think differently than he? His very enrollment in Plainsville High and his subsequent interaction with the many different types of students who make up the Plainsville student body would provide him with at least one such opportunity. Is this not a question of fair play and justice? Can a boy of 17 be blamed for a policy that was formulated and instigated before he was born?

Tom had to admit that much of what Tabbett said made sense to him. But what was "fair" in a case like this? How could he and his brothers in good conscience accept a student like this guy Smith from a country like that? South Africa was the place, after all, where even a champion tennis player like Arthur Ashe wasn't allowed to compete. It was a cinch that they wouldn't accept him—Tom Cosby—as an exchange student in one of their high schools!

Well, nobody could say that all this protesting hadn't brought results. "That's why we're here tonight," he thought.

The meeting was beginning. Mr. Johnson was talking.

". . . opposed to Smith's being enrolled for a year in Plainsville High. Under South Africa's policy of apartheid (which Tom now knew meant complete segregation of people of different races), it would be an implicit endorsement on our part of segregation. Forty percent of our student body would not even be considered for admission to South African secondary schools, let alone be allowed to enroll. The whites in South Africa are a minority who continue to occupy Namibia illegally and without the consent of the black majority. It would be sheer hypocrisy on our part if we were to allow this student to enroll at Plainsville High."

The president of the school board was next. "The official position of the board," he declared, "is to accept any exchange student that any foreign government sends to Plainsville. The board voted last night unanimously to reject the petitions of the NAACP and the various teachers' organizations that Arthur Smith not be allowed to enroll."

A formal invitation had been issued on the part of the Plainsville School Board and endorsed by the mayor. They could not, in good faith, go back on this invitation.

Phyllis Ramires from the state Human Rights Commission spoke next. She spoke in favor of Smith's enrollment. She mentioned such things as the rights of the individual, equal opportunity for all, fair play, and justice as fundamental aspects of American society.

"We should not hold this boy responsible for the actions of his government," she said. "This might be just the opportunity he needs to gain an understanding of what this country stands for, and to open his eyes to the rest of the world."

Now it was Tom's turn. He hadn't been sure as to what he wanted to say. But now he knew. He stepped to the podium and started to speak: "Ladies and gentlemen, I . . .

What should Tom say? What would you say if you were in Tom's shoes? The situation in which Tom finds himself is the kind of situation that all of us are likely to be in at one time or another. Perhaps not exactly like Tom's but quite possibly something fairly similar. How can a teacher proceed to help students determine for themselves what Tom should do? Here are some guidelines to consider:

- Clarify what the value conflict is about.
- Then ask for facts.
- Ask for alternatives.
- Ask for consequences of each alternative.
- Ask for evidence to support the likelihood of each consequence occurring.
- Ask for an evaluation of the desirability of likely consequences.
- Ask for a judgment as to which alternative seems best and why.

Here is a set of questions organized along those lines:

1. What is this incident about? (What is Tom's dilemma?)
2. What might Tom do to try to resolve his dilemma? (What alternatives are open to him?)
3. What might happen to him if he does each of these things? (What might be the consequences of the various alternatives?)
4. What might happen to those who are not immediately involved? (What might be the long- as well as the short-range consequences?)
5. What evidence, if any, is there that these consequences would indeed occur?
6. Would each consequence be good or bad? Why?
7. What do you think Tom should do? (What do you think is the best thing for Tom to do?) Why? (See Figure 6-2)

Question 1 asks students to *sort out and identify what the value conflict or dilemma is about*—what is the disagreement? Is the conflict one of means—that is, a disagreement over how to attain an end or goal that all parties to the conflict regard as desirable, as worth attaining? Or is it a conflict between different ends, with each of the parties to the conflict desiring that a different goal be attained? It is important for everyone involved in the conflict to be clear as to what the conflict is about. Unless there are some agreed-on goals, the discussion cannot proceed.

Once the dilemma has been identified, the facts of the situation must be determined. This is the purpose of question 2. Students are being asked to describe what has happened in the incident. As mentioned previously, this asking for facts is extremely important. It provides students with a solid factual base from which to draw their later conclusions.

Question 2 asks students to *identify alternatives.* It is helpful here to divide the class into small groups of five to six members each. Choose one person in each group to jot down members' ideas and another person to act as chairperson to keep the discussion focused on the task at hand.

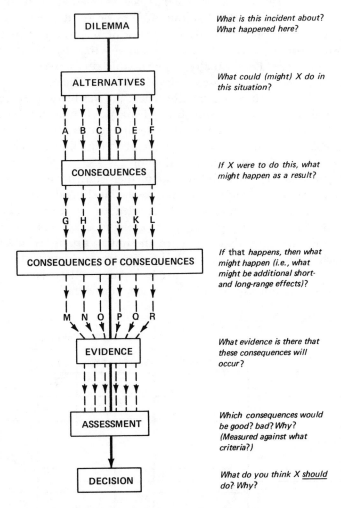

FIGURE 6-2   *Steps involved in analyzing a value dilemma.*

Taken from Jack R. Fraenkel, "Teaching About Values" in Ubbelohde and Fraenkel (ed.), *Values of the American Heritage,* p. 204.

Brainstorm here; encourage students to think of as many things as they can that Tom might possibly say in this situation. Each chairperson should encourage all members of his or her group to suggest ideas, welcoming any and *all* ideas, no matter how farfetched or unusual they may seem at the time.

The next step (questions 3 and 4) is to have the class *predict conse-quences.* What might happen if the alternatives (suggested recommendations) were to become reality? Who would be affected and how? What about effects on future generations?

Consider each alternative that has been suggested (as many as the class is able to handle without getting tired or bored, depending on their age, ability, and so on). Again have the class brainstorm, this time about the possible consequences of each alternative—that is, the things that might happen were Tom actually to pursue this alternative.

As with some other strategies described in this chapter, it is helpful here to prepare a values information chart on the blackboard (or have students prepare such charts in their notebooks). When dealing with value dilemmas, however, the column titles are different from those for value incident charts. Figure 6-3 is one example of a chart that can be used for recording information about a value dilemma.

When students can think of no further consequences, the search begins for evidence to support or refute the likelihood that the consequence would occur. Question 5 is intended to *encourage students to search for data*—reports, photographs, eyewitness accounts, newspaper articles—that describe what happened in similar situations in the past. Once such evidence has been collected, its truthfulness and relevance should be assessed. Are the data that have been collected accurate? Do they refer to situations such as the one under consideration?

FACTS	ALTERNATIVES	CONSEQUENCES			
		SHORT-RANGE		LONG-RANGE	
		Self	Others	Self	Others

FIGURE 6-3   *A values information chart for recording information about a value dilemma.*

When students can find no more evidence, they must consider whether they would *want* each consequence to happen or not. They also should be encouraged to discuss why they think certain consequences are more desirable than others. Question 6 will help students *ascertain whether each consequence is good or bad.*

It is necessary at this point, therefore, to make sure that students understand the concept of criteria. A *criterion* is the characteristic (or set of characteristics) that *makes* a consequence (or anything else) desirable or undesirable (or somewhere in between). Criteria are essential for intelligent, reasoned ranking. Value objects (such as ideas, policies, individuals) often are rated quite differently, because the people doing the rating are using different sets of criteria. The development of criteria is an extremely important task. It not only gives students a yardstick or guideline against which to measure things (e.g., consequences) to determine their desirability or undesirability but also enables other students to understand the reasons for the rating, whatever it may be.

Students must do the determining, however. It does not help students to think about what criteria are important if the teacher simply tells them what criteria to use. But the teacher can and should expose students to a wide variety of criteria so that they do not look at consequences from only one point of view. Thus, various criteria should be identified and their meaning discussed with the class. Such criteria include:

- The *moral* criterion. (To what extent would the lives and dignity of human beings be enhanced or diminished?)
- The *legal* criterion. (Would any laws be broken?)
- The *aesthetic* criterion. (Would the beauty of something be increased or reduced?)
- The *ecological* criterion. (Would the natural environment be harmed or helped?)
- The *economic* criterion. (How much cost would be involved? Are sufficient funds available to meet these costs?)
- The *health and safety* criterion. (Would the lives of human beings be endangered in any way?)

These are only some of many possible criteria students can use. They should also be encouraged to suggest additional criteria for consideration. It is important to realize that any sort of reasoned, intelligent rating of consequences (or of anything else) in terms of desirability/undesirability is impossible unless *some* criteria are used. To help students analyze consequences from several different points of view, a value analysis chart can be used (see Figure 6-4).

Class members should finish discussing the desirability of each conse-

ALTERNATIVES OPEN TO TOM	CONSEQUENCES	DESIRABILITY FROM VARIOUS POINTS OF VIEW							RANKING
		Moral	Legal	Aesthetic	Ecological	Economic	Health and safety	Etc.	

FIGURE 6-4   A value-analysis chart for considering the desirability of consequences from different points of view.

quence and state their reasons and listen to those of others for considering certain consequences either desirable or undesirable. Then the choices open to Tom Cosby can be ranked from most desirable to least desirable by the students, using the last column on the right in the value analysis chart. At this point question 7 can be discussed—*What do you think Tom should do?*

Most students in the class should now be able to discuss the following: Why did they rank the alternatives as they did? Which alternatives seemed most preferred? Why? Would the reasons given for considering a particular alternative most desirable in this situation hold true in other situations as well? Why or why not?

Underlying this strategy is the assumption that through realizing, discussing, and evaluating various courses of action, along with the consequences of these alternatives, and the evidence to support or refute the likelihood of their occurrence, three things will happen:

- Students will become more aware that all people hold values that conflict sometimes.
- Students will realize that there are many different sets of criteria that can be used to evaluate a consequence.
- Students, we hope, will become more willing to evaluate the consequences of the different courses of action to which they now have been exposed from several points of view.

In all the strategies presented in this and the previous chapter, the nature of the *content* students are asked to discuss is very important—that is, the issue or topic around which the value incident or value dilemma revolves. Interest, readability, realism—all are important characteristics of value incidents and value dilemmas. It also is important, however, to

"Thinking doesn't hurt as much as I thought it would."

Source: Reg Hider from *Today's Education,* March 1972, p. 17. Reprinted by permission of National Education Association.

vary the type of incident and dilemma students are asked to explore and discuss so as to prevent boredom. A few words about the nature and sequencing of value-oriented subject matter follow.

    Some suggestions about the sequencing of value dilemmas were made in Chapter 4 (see page 79), and they apply to value incidents as well. The important thing is (1) to present students with incidents and dilemmas that involve a variety of such value-related concepts as fairness, obligation, conscience, responsibility, duty, courage, and honor; and (2) to vary the *range of applicability* of these incidents and dilemmas by insuring that they involve decisions and choices that affect larger and larger groups of people, including organizations (e.g., multinational corporations), governments, international agencies, and even planet Earth as a whole. The particular dilemmas and incidents to which students should be exposed depend on their age, level of sophistication, and ability. A conscientious attempt should be made, however (given these limiting factors) to help them explore and discuss situations that are increasingly more difficult, complex, and long-range in terms of their possible effects (see Figure 6-5).

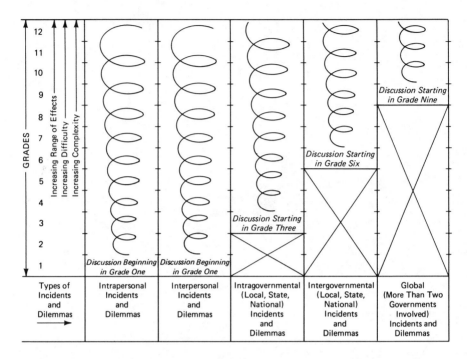

FIGURE 6-5   *One possible way of sequencing the exploration and discussion of value incidents and value dilemmas.*

1. "A realization that values often conflict may help students to understand why people are often inconsistent in their behavior." How would such understanding be of benefit to students?

2. What do you think is Tom Cosby's dilemma? If you were Tom, how would you resolve the dilemma?

3. What other criteria, besides those identified on page 133, might be important to consider in evaluating consequences? Why?

4. Would it be possible for people to come up with the same evaluation of a consequence if they used different sets of criteria? Why or why not?

THE TEACHER AS MODEL

In Chapter 5 the importance of developing a rationale to help guide decisions about values education was discussed briefly. Another advantage of having a rationale is that it can help teachers think about and evaluate the kinds of examples they set for students. This is an important piece of analysis for all teachers to make, for it is a rather commonplace observation that children imitate the behavior of other children and of adults. Many social learning or behaviorally oriented psychologists argue, in fact, that students acquire their values to a large extent through observing and imitating both peer and adult models.

Liebert has shown, for example, that observation of aggressive peers, adults, and even cartoon characters can increase swiftly the amount of aggression that children express in their play.[6]

Bandura and his associates describe their study in which three groups of nursery school children were shown a film of an adult model striking, kicking, and punching an inflated "Bobo" doll that was the same size as the adult. One group then saw the adult model rewarded; the second group saw the model punished; and the third group saw the model treated neutrally (i.e., neither rewarded nor punished). In the reward situation, a second adult gave the model a treat (7-Up, popcorn, or candy) for his "superb aggressive performance." In the punishment situation, the second adult—among other things—shook his finger at the model and remarked, "Hey there, you big bully. Quit picking on that clown! I won't tolerate it." When the model was treated neutrally, no second adult appeared.

When the children were left alone with the doll, those who had seen the model punished displayed a lesser number of aggressive acts than did the children in the other two groups. Later, however, when they were offered prizes if they would reproduce the model's behavior, they were able to do so. They had learned the model's aggressive behaviors, even though they had not immediately performed them after observing the model.[7]

Mischel and Liebert conducted a study in which two groups of children each were placed in game situations with an adult. Each child had to determine a level or standard of performance by which he or she would abide. In one group, the adult consistently preached and practiced a stringent standard. In the second group, the adult was inconsistent; he still *preached* a stringent standard but actually *displayed* a much more lenient one in front of the children.

As long as the adults were present, the behavior of the children in the two groups did not differ. They continued to adhere to the stringent standard the adult had imposed. However, when the children were left alone (and secretly observed through one-way mirrors), many of those who had observed the inconsistent adult lowered their standards. But none of those taught by the consistent adult lowered theirs. Furthermore, those

6 R. M. Liebert, "Television and Social Learning: Some Relationships Between Viewing Violence and Behaving Aggressively," in J. P. Murray, E. A. Rubenstein, and G. A. Comstock, eds., *Television and Social Behavior,* Vol. II: *Television and Social Learning* (Washington, D.C.: Government Printing Office, 1972).

7 Albert Bandura, "Influence of Models' Reinforcement Contingencies on the Acquisition of Imitative Responses," *Journal of Personality and Social Psychology,* 1, 1965, pp. 589–595.

children taught by the inconsistent adult were more likely to demonstrate a lower standard in the presence of other children and even to recommend such lower standards to their peers.[8]

In real life, of course, children see the behavior of a variety of peers, teachers, and other adults. What effects does exposure to such a variety of models have? Liebert and several of his associates conducted a series of studies seeking answers to just this question of multiple modeling.[9] They suggest two general principles they believe are supported by the results of the studies.

An expressed rule is:

1. increasingly more likely to be broken by a child as the number of other individuals whom he or she sees break the rule increases;
2. increasingly more likely to be followed by a child as the number of others whom he or she sees follow the rule increases.

These principles re-emphasize the importance of teachers becoming clear about their own values and thinking about whether or not their actions and sayings reflect those values.

It is especially important for teachers to think about what they say and do as they interact with students in discussions about values. Put-downs, abruptness, disapproval of a student's ideas, failing to encourage shy or hesitant individuals to express themselves, failing to prevent monopolization of a discussion by a few students, ridiculing value judgments with which he or she disagrees (or allowing students to do this) —all such actions by a teacher are almost guaranteed to discourage students from making and discussing inferences about values. On the other hand, encouragement, interest in what all students have to say, acceptance of divergent or unusual opinions, curiosity, friendliness, and similar behaviors and attitudes are likely to encourage and prolong such discussions. Here are a few other suggestions.[10]

Accept all statements that students offer, no matter how silly or

[8] W. Mischel and R. M. Liebert, "Effects of Discrepancies Between Observed and Imposed Reward Criteria on Their Acquisition and Transmission," *Journal of Personality and Social Psychology*, Vol. 3, 1966, pp. 45–53.

[9] J. H. Hill and R. M. Liebert, "Effects of Consistent or Deviant Modeling Cues on the Adoption of a Self-Imposed Standard," *Psychonomic Science*, 13, 1968, 243–244; M. J. McMains and R. M. Liebert, "The Influence of Discrepancies Between Successively Modeled Self-Reward Criteria on the Adoption of a Self-Imposed Standard," *Journal of Personality and Social Psychology*, 8, 1968, 166–171; R. M. Liebert and L. E. Fernandez, "Effects of Single and Multiple Modeling Cues on Establishing Norms for Sharing," *Proceedings, 78th Annual Convention,* American Psychological Association, 1970.

[10] Jack R. Fraenkel, "Inquiry into Values," in M. Eugene Gilliom, ed., *Practical Methods for the Social Studies*. (Belmont, Calif.: Wadsworth Publishing Co., 1977).

unusual they may seem when first presented. This does not mean that you must *agree* with what a student says, only that you should not reject it out of hand. Such acceptance can be accomplished by responding in a somewhat noncommittal manner (e.g., by saying, "I see," "I understand," or simply, "Okay").

Do not require students to talk if they do not want to. The following example illustrates a teacher's willingness to respect a student's desire not to comment on a particular issue.

> T: We've been talking the last few days about the issue of morality in government and in particular the question of what a government official should do when his principles come into conflict with what he perceives to be his responsibility to his constituents. Sam, you said yesterday that you felt this same dilemma was one that many military officers had to face when their principles came into conflict with their responsibilities as officers. Can you give us an example to help us understand your reasoning here?

> Sam: Well, I mean. Like, for example, a good officer is supposed to follow orders. But what if he feels that an order he's been given is a bad order—I mean, you know, it will really hurt a lot of people if he carries it out. He has got a real tough decision to make.

> T: What do you think an officer should do if he finds himself in that kind of situation?

> Sam: I guess I think he has to stand by his principles.

> Roger: I don't agree. Orders are orders, and it's a soldier's duty to obey them.

> T: Always?

> Roger: Yeah, otherwise an army can't survive.

> T: Let's get some other ideas here, too. Phil, what's your opinion of all this?

> Phil: I don't think I have one right now.

> T: Okay. But if you get an idea or two later on, don't hesitate to let us know.

When a student is having trouble getting his thoughts out, it sometimes is helpful to restate what he has expressed without indicating approval or disapproval of his ideas, as in the following illustration:

> S: When I graduated from eighth grade—uh—my family moved to a new place, er, town—uh—in the summer and I had to start—uh, begin high school there. I didn't know any of the kids and I didn't —uh—feel very easy when school started.

> T: You felt kind of uncomfortable?

S: I sure did. It was pretty painful.

T: I can understand why you'd feel that way.

Let students know that you want them to offer their ideas by telling them so. This is how one teacher indicated to his class that he wanted to hear what his students thought:

Racquel: I don't know much about this, anyway.

T: I'd really like to hear what you think, Racquel.

Racquel: Well, it doesn't seem fair to me that only seniors should get to go into the inner courtyard to eat their lunch. This school is supposed to be for everybody, isn't it? All students should get to use the inner courtyard, and it shouldn't be a special privilege for you to have just because you're a senior.

T: If I understand you, you're saying that it isn't fair for seniors to have the inner courtyard reserved for them as some sort of special privilege.

Racquel: Yes, I am.

T: I see.

Take care not to impose your views on students. If discussions are to prosper, the teacher must encourage consideration and reflection upon all ideas that are offered, including his own. A helpful procedure here is to prepare on the blackboard, or in some other highly visible spot, a three column chart such as the one below.

Statements	Evidence to Support	Evidence to Refute

Students now can be encouraged to locate and record in the appropriate columns facts that provide evidence to support or refute particular ideas.

Don't hesitate to introduce ideas contrary to those expressed by students in order to bring out other aspects of an issue. Make sure, however, that students realize you are not implying that these are necessarily *"the"* best ideas, nor demanding that they accept them. The introduction of contradictory ideas is perfectly justified as a technique to promote discussion and to help students expand their awareness of people's feelings about a values issue. Insisting that students accept your ideas is not only unjust but also contradicts the reflective examination of various ideas. Here is an example of how one teacher tried to encourage students to consider an idea rather than dismissing it without thinking about it:

T: You have all suggested various things that you think might contribute to decreasing the likelihood of nuclear war in the future. One thing that nobody has mentioned is the possibility that the United States should begin the process by destroying all of its nuclear weapons over a five-year period and inviting all the other nuclear powers then to follow suit.

S: Are you kidding? The Russians would have a fantastic weapons and power edge on us.

S: Are you really in favor of that?

T: I am not saying that I am either in favor of or opposed to the idea. I am simply suggesting that it might be an idea worth looking at. There are some pretty intelligent people in favor of this idea, and I think we should consider it.

There is no question that children are influenced by and often imitate the behavior of adult and peer models. It is for this reason that teachers need to consider whether the behaviors they themselves display are the sorts of behaviors they want their students to emulate.

"Good grief! What kind of example are we gonna set—
same again, son—for our young . . . ?"

Source: Yardley Jones—*Toronto Telegram,* Canada (Rothco).

---

1. Students will be exposed to many models (teachers, parents, peers, other adults) during the course of their schooling. These models are likely to differ con-

siderably in the behaviors they demonstrate. What would you say to a student who comments on this fact?

2. Here are some examples of justifications given by various people for saying one thing, yet doing another: a) when the conditions under which a person originally makes a statement no longer apply; b) when an individual or his family is in considerable danger of life and limb; or c) when someone has acquired new information that now makes it appear likely that others will be harmed if he or she follows through on earlier statements. Would you agree that these reasons are justifiable ones for being inconsistent? Why or why not?

TELLING OTHERS WHAT TO VALUE

There is one type of behavior in particular, however, that teachers would be well advised to avoid. This is the practice of telling other people what sorts of things they should value—particularly through the use of such techniques as arousing fear about the consequences of certain acts, appeals to conscience, or the citing of "good examples" from history and literature. Material containing supposedly inspirational slogans, unequivocal statements as to what is right or wrong, and warnings about the dangers that can befall those who are not honest and trustworthy likewise should be avoided.

The McGuffy readers used in most schools during the nineteenth century are perhaps the most famous examples of such materials. One used a picture accompanying story of two children who disobeyed their mother by crossing a pond when the ice was soft, then fell into the freezing water and almost drowned. Thankful for their close escape, the penitent children confessed their "sin" to their mother and "never forgot the lesson they learned." This story was typical of much of the literature in schoolbooks of the period, in which those who did not respect and obey authority suffered dire consequences.

The problem with materials and techniques of this sort is that they are, for the most part, not very effective. Though much depends on the nature and manner of the appeal, reliance on such techniques to convince young people that something has merit or is worth doing just doesn't work for most. This also applies to verbal appeals to conscience and to citing outstanding men and women from history and works of literature. Our prisons are filled with thousands of individuals whose parents repeatedly told them when they were young to "be good."

Almost fifty years ago, Hartshorne and May found out that didactic forms of instruction had no effect on moral conduct, as measured by the degree to which experimental subjects in various character education classes and religious instruction programs cheated.

"Oh, my teacher and I communicate,
all right . . . she looks at me a
certain way and I understand
what I'd better do!"

Source: *Today's Education,* December 1970, p. 52. Reprinted by permission of the National Education Association.

The learning of verbal rules about honesty had no relation to how the subjects acted. Those who cheated expressed as much or more moral disapproval of cheating as those who did not cheat. The decision to cheat, it appeared, was largely determined by expediency, depending on the degree of risk and effort involved.[11]

Festinger describes a study in which fear-arousing elements were introduced during training in oral hygiene. High school students were divided into four groups; three of the groups heard appeals that attempted to persuade them to use proper methods of oral hygiene. The appeals were characterized as strong, moderate, and minimal. The strong appeal contained fear-arousing elements; the other two were more objective presentations. There were follow-up questionnaires to determine how many students had changed their practices to conform to the recommended methods. The relations between behavior and the degree to which students were made to feel concerned about oral hygiene were actually *in the reverse direction* from what one would expect in any simple relation-

[11] H. Hartshorne and M. A. May, *Studies in the Nature of Character: Studies in Deceit,* Vol. I (New York: Macmillan, 1928).

ship between attitude change and behavior. Festinger summed up his findings as follows: "All in all, we can detect no effect on behavior or *even a clear and persistent change in opinion* brought about by a persuasive communication [italics added]." [12]

The use of such techniques as appeals to conscience, rewards and punishment, and the citing of "good examples" often is referred to as *moralizing.* Moralizing frequently is equated with a sort of mindless preaching, but this is unfair. Moralizing *can* be defined as "to point out the moral in or draw a moral from" an incident or story or even "to improve the morals of" students. Its primary definition, however, is "to think, write, or speak about matters of right and wrong." The value and acceptability of moralizing, therefore, really depends on the *manner* in which it occurs. Teachers or other authority figures can simply *tell* students to accept their conclusions that a particular thing (object, policy, way of behaving) is good or right because they say it is, without giving any reasons for their conclusions. This does not appear in most cases to be very effective. On the other hand, they can teach students to *seek out the reasons* behind recommendations. Why are advocates of a particular policy recommending it? What consequences do they say will result from following it? What evidence is there that such consequences have happened elsewhere?

When students are taught (even if only by implication) to accept the conclusions of authority figures without qualification, they later may have trouble dealing with any criticisms of such conclusions. When the conclusions of one authority conflict with the conclusions of other authorities, many adults do not know what to do. Since they learned in school only to accept, rather than to assess, conclusions, they now are unable to choose intelligently from among them.

---

1. The use of such techniques as appeals to conscience, slogans, and warnings is said by some observers to be a rather commonplace occurrence in many schools. If this is true, how would you explain it?

2. Might there be times when a teacher *would* be well advised to tell his or her students what they should value? If so, when?

3. Would you agree that the value of moralizing depends on the manner in which it occurs? Why or why not?

4. Look up a definition of moralizing in a dictionary. Of the definitions listed, which one(s) do you think would be the most commonly accepted by most people? Why?

5. Are there any times when a teacher would be justified in asking his or her students to accept the teacher's conclusions without question? Why or why not?

---

[12] Leon Festinger, "Behavioral Support for Opinion Change," *Public Opinion Quarterly*, 28, Fall 1964, pp. 404–417.

SOME CONCLUDING THOUGHTS

The ideas presented here and in the previous chapters are by no means all there is to say about values education.[13] Rather, this book outlines some fairly simple strategies and procedures teachers can use to help students analyze (that is, think about and discuss) values and value issues in their classrooms. And it points out some of the limitations of the values clarification and discussion-of-moral-dilemmas approaches.

The discussion of value incidents and value dilemmas is certainly not all there is to teaching about values. Many other ideas and techniques such as value surveys, simulation games, interviewing people about what they consider important, making films, composing songs, poems, or photographic essays having to do with values; cross-age tutoring, essays and reports on values, working in a political campaign, or participating in community affairs offer considerable potential for educating young people in values. All should be considered by anyone interested in values education.

A discussion and analysis of these ideas and techniques, however, is beyond the scope of this book; that must wait for another time and another book. At present, what techniques to use, what skills to stress, and/or what subject matter to study remain pretty much of an open question. To be sure, a few techniques such as the use of values clarification activities and the discussion of moral dilemmas are currently fashionable. But there is no valid evidence that these techniques are any *better* than others not in fashion in achieving any sort of short-range or long-range intellectual or emotional development in students. We still need lots of models and strategies having to do with the development of values proposed, along with lots of research that tests and compares these models and strategies in terms of effectiveness in effecting such emotional and intellectual development.

It is a rather discouraging fact that there is little agreement among educators today as to what values education even involves. Although the topic is a favorite one at conventions and workshops and although numerous books and articles on the subject continue to appear, there is

[13] See Douglas P. Superka, et al., *Values Education Sourcebook: Conceptual Approches, Materials Analyses, and an Annotated Bibliography* (Boulder, Colo.: ERIC Clearinghouse for Social Studies/Social Science Education and Social Science Education Consortium, 1976) for a description of a number of approaches to values education.

not much consensus as to what being "educated in values" means.[14] So as a final note, here are a few questions that I think should be considered by all persons interested in developing any sort of comprehensive program of values education in the schools.

1. What does being "educated in values" involve? (What sorts of skills, attitudes, knowledge, and so on does someone so educated possess that others not so educated do not?)
2. What sorts of subject matter should students study? And why? How should this subject matter be presented? And when?
3. In what sorts of learning activities should students participate? How often should they participate in these activities? And why?
4. When should such a program begin? And how long should it last?
5. What skills would teachers need to develop to help students become educated in values? How can they acquire these skills?
6. How should we measure progress or growth in values education?

There are, no doubt, many other questions that can and should be asked. But our first task is to become much clearer as to what we are after. What kinds of individuals do we want to help develop? What are our goals when it comes to values? Just what *does* values education involve? Once we become really clear about what we want and where we're going, answers to some of the other questions listed above should suggest themselves. When our goals are clear, ways to attain these goals and to assess progress toward them should be much easier to determine.

EXERCISES

1. Here are some objectives that have been proposed by various value educators. How many would you endorse? What is your rationale for approval or disapproval?

a. To define the term "value."
b. To know what a value indicator is.
c. To appreciate the values of other people.
d. To make reasoned inferences about the values of others.
e. To know what is good, right, and beautiful.
f. To formulate some idea about what is good, right, and beautiful.
g. To participate in discussions of valued things.
h. To analyze value judgments.

[14] A notable exception to this lack of clarity is the recent work by Shaver and Strong. See James P. Shaver and William Strong, *Facing Value Decisions: Rationale-Building for Teachers.* (Belmont, Calif.: Wadsworth Publishing Co., 1976).

    i. To clarify one's own values.

    j. To realize that values conflict.

    k. To learn what human beings have valued over time.

    l. To learn what values have endured through the centuries.

    m. To explore feelings.

    n. To explore and evaluate alternatives and consequences in value conflict situations.

2. Listed below are a number of value judgments, some of which are definitional and some propositional. See if you can identify which ones are which.

    a. That is a very dependable stapler.

    b. She has the best backhand of any person on the team.

    c. Personal property taxes in the city of San Francisco should be lowered.

    d. Drinking to excess is bad for a person's health.

    e. An electric drill that takes a $\frac{3}{8}$-inch bit is more useful than one that takes only a $\frac{1}{4}$-inch bit.

    f. Bud's ice cream is a lot better tasting than Howard Johnson's.

    g. If we want to improve the quality of the teaching profession, we should pay beginning teachers higher salaries.

    h. He's the finest lawyer in the state.

    i. The United States government should cease giving aid to dictatorships if it wishes to maintain the respect of its allies.

    j. The United Nations ought to have its own police force.

    k. "You shouldn't have signed that agreement, Harry!"

3. Discuss "Tom Cosby's Dilemma" with some other people to see how they would resolve the dilemma. At what level of moral reasoning (see page 56) would you place their responses?

4. See if you can write some value dilemmas yourself. What difficulties do you encounter? Now try to write some value incidents. Which is harder to prepare?

5. In Chapter 4, I suggested presenting students with several alternative ways of resolving a particular dilemma—with each alternative reflecting a different level of moral reasoning—as another way to foster the development of higher-level moral reasoning. See if you can suggest an alternative that reflects each of Kohlberg's six levels to resolve Tom Cosby's dilemma. Ask some of your friends or classmates to see if they can do the same. Be sure first that they are familiar with the six levels of moral reasoning that Kohlberg has suggested, however. Then compare the various alternatives without letting each other know what level of reasoning each is intended to represent. What sort of agreement do you find?

6. Observe some teachers in action. What sorts of models do they present for their students? How consistent are they in what they say and what they do?

7. Listed below are a number of objectives either suggested or implied herein as important components of values education. Which of these would you say is most important? Least important? Why? What others would you add?

- The clarification of one's personal commitments.
- The development of moral reasoning.
- The making of reasoned inferences about values.
- The comparison of one's own values with the values of other people.
- The evaluation of value judgments.
- The definition of value terms.
- The identificaion of alternative solutions to problems.
- The consideration of consequences.
- The building of empathy.

BIBLIOGRAPHY

ALLPORT, GORDON W. *The Nature of Prejudice.* Reading, Mass.: Addison-Wesley, 1954.

ALSCHULER, ALFRED, DIANE TABOR, and JAMES MCINTYRE. *Teaching Achievement Motivation.* Middletown, Conn.: Education Ventures, 1971.

ALSTON, W. P. "Comments on Kohlberg's 'From Is to Ought,'" in T. Mischel (ed.), *Cognitive Development and Epistemology.* New York: Academic Press, 1971, pp. 269–284.

ALTSHULER, THELMA. *Choices.* Englewood Cliffs, N.J.: Prentice-Hall, 1970.

BANDURA, ALBERT. "Influence of Models: Reinforcement Contingencies on the Acquisition of Imitative Responses," *Journal of Personality and Social Psychology,* 1, 1965, pp. 589–595.

BARR, ROBERT D. (ed.). *Values and Youth.* Washington, D.C.: National Council for the Social Studies, 1971.

BARTHOLOMEW, PAUL C. *Leading Cases on the Constitution.* Totowa, N.J.: Littlefield, Adams, 1968.

BECK, CLIVE. *Moral Education in the Schools.* Toronto: Ontario Institute for Studies in Education, 1971.

BELOK, MICHAEL, et al. *Approaches to Values in Education.* Dubuque, Iowa: W. C. Brown, 1966.

BEYER, BARRY K. "Conducting Moral Discussions in the Classroom," *Social Education,* April 1976, pp. 194–202.

BRONFENBRENNER, URIE. *Two Worlds of Childhood.* New York: Russell Sage Foundation, 1970.

BROUDY, HARRY S. *Enlightened Cherishing: An Essay on Aesthetic Education.* Urbana, Ill.: University of Illinois Press, 1972.

BROUDY, HARRY S., B. OTHANEL SMITH, and JOE R. BURNETT. *Democracy and Excellence in American Secondary Education.* Chicago: Rand McNally, 1964.

BULL, NORMAN J. *Moral Judgment from Childhood to Adolescence.* London: Routledge and Kegan Paul, 1969.

CANNING, JEREMIAH (ed.). *Values in an Age of Confrontation.* Columbus, Ohio: Charles E. Merrill, 1970.

CASTEEL, J. DOYLE, and ROBERT J. STAHL. *Value Clarification in the Classroom: A Primer.* Pacific Palisades, Calif.: Goodyear, 1975.

CHASE, LARRY. *The Other Side of the Report Card: A How-to-Do-It Program for Affective Education.* Pacific Palisades, Calif.: Goodyear, 1975.

CHESLER, MARK, and ROBERT FOX. *Role-Playing Methods in the Classroom.* Chicago: Science Research Associates, 1966.

CHILDS, JOHN L. *Education and Morals.* New York: Appleton-Century-Crofts, 1950.

"Conscience and War: The Moral Dilemma," *Intercom,* November/December, 1969.

CURWIN, RICHARD L., and BARBARA SCHNEIDER FUHRMANN. *Discovering Your Teaching Self.* Englewood Cliffs, N.J.: Prentice-Hall, 1975.

DECECCIO, JOHN P., and ARLENE K. RICHARDS. *Growing Pains: Uses of School Conflict.* New York: Aberdeen Press, 1974.

DEWEY, JOHN. *Democracy and Education: An Introduction to the Philosophy of Education.* New York: Macmillan, 1916 (paperback edition, 1961).

DEWEY, JOHN, and JAMES H. TUFTS. *Ethics.* New York: Henry Holt & Company, 1932, revised edition. Also see the first edition of 1908.

DUSKA, RONALD, and MARIELLEN WHELAN. *Moral Development: A Guide to Paiget and Kohlberg.* New York: Paulist Press, 1975.

Educational Psychology: A Contemporary View. Del Mar, Calif.: Communications Research Machines, 1973.

EHMAN, LEE, HOWARD MEHLINGER, and JOHN PATRICK. *Toward Effective Instruction in Secondary Social Studies.* Boston: Houghton Mifflin, 1974.

ENNIS, ROBERT H. *Logic in Teaching.* Englewood Cliffs, N.J.: Prentice-Hall, 1969.

FENTON, EDWIN. "Moral Education: The Research Findings," *Social Education,* April 1976, pp. 188–193.

FERGUSON, PATRICK, and JOHN FRIESEN. "Values Theory and Teaching: The Problems of Autonomy versus Determinism," *Theory and Research in Social Education,* December 1974, pp. 1–24.

FESTINGER, LEON. "Behavioral Support for Opinion Change," *Public Opinion Quarterly,* 28, Fall 1964, pp. 404–417.

FLAVELL, J. H. *The Developmental Psychology of Jean Piaget.* Princeton, N.J.: Van Nostrand, 1963.

FOTION, N. *Moral Situations.* Kent, Ohio: Kent State University Press, 1968.

FRAENKEL, JACK R. "Value Education in the Social Studies," *Phi Delta Kappan,* April 1969, pp. 457–462.

FRAENKEL, JACK R. *Helping Students Think and Value: Strategies for Teaching the Social Studies.* Englewood Cliffs, N.J.: Prentice-Hall, 1973.

FRAENKEL, JACK R. "Strategies for Developing Values," *Today's Education,* November/December 1973, pp. 49–55.

FRAENKEL, JACK R. "The Importance of Learning Activities," *Social Education,* November 1973, pp. 674–678.

FRAENKEL, JACK R. "The Kohlberg Bandwagon: Some Reservations," *Social Education,* April 1976, pp. 216–222.

FRAENKEL, JACK R. "Inquiry into Values," in M. Eugene Gilliom (ed.), *Practical Methods for the Social Studies.* Belmont, Calif.: Wadsworth, 1977.

FRAENKEL, JACK R., MARGARET CARTER, and BETTY REARDON. *The Struggle for Human Rights.* New York: Random House, 1974.

FRANKENA, W. K. *Ethics.* Englewood Cliffs, N.J.: Prentice-Hall, 1963.

GALBRAITH, RONALD E., and THOMAS M. JONES. "Teaching Strategies for Moral Dilemmas: An Application of Kohlberg's Theory of Moral Development to the Social Studies Classroom," *Social Education,* January 1975, pp. 16–22.

GALBRAITH, RONALD E., and THOMAS M. JONES. *Moral Reasoning: A Teaching Handbook for Adapting Kohlberg to the Classroom.* Anoka, Minn.: Greenhaven Press, 1976.

GILLIOM, EUGENE (ed.). *Practical Methods for the Social Studies.* Belmont, Calif.: Wadsworth, 1977.

GLASSER, WILLIAM. *Schools Without Failure.* New York: Harper and Row, 1969.

GREENBERG, HERBERT M. *Teaching with Feeling.* New York: Macmillan, 1969.

HARE, R. M. *Freedom and Reason.* New York: Oxford University Press, 1965.

HARMIN, MERRILL, HOWARD KIRSCHENBAUM, and SIDNEY B. SIMON. *Clarifying Values Through Subject Matter: Applications for the Classroom.* Minneapolis: Winston Press, 1973.

HARTOONIAN, H. MICHAEL. "A Disclosure Approach to Value Analysis in Social Studies Education: Rationale and Components," *Theory and Research in Social Education,* October 1973. pp. 1–26.

HAWLEY, ROBERT C. *Value Exploration Through Role Playing: Practical Strategies for Use in the Classroom.* New York: Hart, 1975.

HILL, J. H., and R. M. LIEBERT. "Effects of Consistent or Deviant Modeling Cues on the Adoption of a Self-Imposed Standard," *Psychonomic Science,* 13, 1968, pp. 243–244.

HODGKINSON, HAROLD L. *Education, Interaction, and Social Change.* Englewood Cliffs, N.J.: Prentice-Hall, 1967.

HOLSTEIN, C. "Moral Judgment Change in Early Adolescence and Middle Age: A Longitudinal Study," unpublished paper, 1973.

HOWE, LELAND W., and MARY MARTHA HOWE. *Personalizing Education: Values Clarification and Beyond.* New York: Hart, 1975.

HUNT, MAURICE P. *Foundations of Education: Social and Cultural Perspectives.* New York: Holt, Rinehart and Winston, 1975.

HUNT, MAURICE P., and LAWRENCE E. METCALF. *Teaching High School Social Studies.* New York: Harper and Row, 1968.

INLOW, GAIL M. *Values in Transition.* New York: John Wiley & Sons, 1972.

KIRSCHENBAUM, HOWARD, and SIDNEY B. SIMON (eds.). *Readings in Values Clarification.* Minneapolis: Winston Press, 1973.

KOOHLBERG, LAWRENCE. "Moral Education in the Schools: A Developmental View," *School Review,* Spring 1966.

KOHLBERG, LAWRENCE. "Stage and Sequence: The Cognitive-Developmental Approach to Socialization," in D. Goslin (ed.), *Handbook of Socialization Theory and Research.* Chicago: Rand McNally, 1969.

KOHLBERG, LAWRENCE. "Education for Justice: A Modern Statement of the

Platonic View," in N. F. Sizer and T. R. Sizer (eds.), *Moral Education.* Cambridge, Mass.: Harvard University Press, 1970.

KOHLBERG, LAWRENCE. "The Concepts of Developmental Psychology and the Central Guide to Education: Examples from Cognitive, Moral and Psychological Education," in *The Proceedings of the Conference on Psychology and the Process of Schooling in the Next Decade: Alternative Conceptions.* Minneapolis: University of Minnesota Audio-Visual Extension, 1971, pp. 1–55.

KOHLBERG, LAWRENCE. "From Is to Ought: How to Commit the Naturalistic Fallacy and Get Away With It in the Study of Moral Development," in T. Mischel (ed.), *Cognitive Development and Epistemology.* New York: Academic Press, 1971.

KOHLBERG, LAWRENCE. "Stages of Moral Development as a Basis for Moral Education," in C. M. Beck, B. S. Crittenden, and E. U. Sullivan (eds.), *Moral Education: Interdisciplinary Approaches.* Toronto: University of Toronto Press, 1971.

KOHLBERG, LAWRENCE. "Indoctrination versus Relativity in Value Education," *Zygon,* 1972, pp. 285–310.

KOHLBERG, LAWRENCE. "The Cognitive-Developmental Approach to Moral Education," *Phi Delta Kappan,* June 1975, pp. 670–677.

KOHLBERG, LAWRENCE, and CAROL GILLIGAN. "The Adolescent as a Philosopher: The Discovery of the Self in a Postconventional World," *Daedalus,* 1971, pp. 1051–1085.

KOHLBERG, LAWRENCE, and R. KRAMER. "Continuities and Discontinuities in Childhood and Adult Moral Development," *Human Development,* 1969, pp. 93–120.

KRATHWOHL, D. R., BENJAMIN S. BLOOM, and BERTRAM B. MASIA. *Taxonomy of Educational Objectives: Affective Domain.* New York: David McKay, 1964.

KURTINES, WILLIAM, and ESTHER, B. GRIEF. "The Development of Moral Thought: Review and Evaluation of Kohlberg's Approach," *Psychological Bulletin,* August 1974, pp. 453–470.

LIEBERT, R. M. "Television and Social Learning: Some Relationships Between Viewing Violence and Behaving Aggressively," in J. P. Murray, E. A. Rubenstein, and G. A. Comstock (eds.), *Television and Social Behavior, Vol. II: Television and Social Learning.* Washington, D.C.: Government Printing Office, 1972.

LIEBERT, R. M., and L. E. FERNANDEZ. "Effects of Single and Multiple Modeling Cues on Establishing Norms for Sharing," *Proceedings, 78th Annual Convention,* American Psychology Association, 1970.

LIKONA, THOMAS (ed.). *Morality: Theory, Research, and Social Issues.* New York: Holt, Rinehart, and Winston, 1976.

LOCKWOOD, ALAN. *Moral Reasoning: The Value of Life.* Middletown, Conn.: Xerox, 1972.

McMAINS, M. J., and R. M. LIEBERT. "The Influence of Discrepancies Between Successively Modeled Self-Reward Criteria on the Adoption of a Self-Imposed Standard," *Journal of Personality and Social Psychology,* 8, 1968, pp. 166–171.

MARLER, CHARLES D. *Philosophy and Schooling.* Boston: Allyn & Bacon, 1975.

MASSIALAS, BYRON G., NANCY F. SPRAGUE, and JOSEPH B. HURST. *Social Issues*

Through Inquiry: Coping in an Age of Crises. Englewood Cliffs, N.J.: Prentice-Hall, 1975.

MEANS, RICHARD L. The Ethical Imperative: *The Crisis in American Values.* Garden City, N.Y.: Doubleday, 1969.

METCALF, LAWRENCE E. (ed.). *Values Education: Rationale, Strategies, and Procedures.* Washington, D.C.: National Council for the Social Studies (41st Yearbook), 1971.

MEYER, JOHN R., BRIAN BURNHAM, and JOHN CHOLVAT (eds.). *Values Education: Theory/Practice/Problems/Prospects.* Waterloo, Ontario, Canada: Wilfrid Laurie, 1975.

MICHAELIS, JOHN V. *Social Studies for Children in a Democracy,* 6th ed. Englewood Cliffs, N.J.: Prentice-Hall, 1976.

MORRIS, VAN CLEVE, and YOUNG PAI. *Philosophy and the American School.* Boston: Houghton Mifflin, 1976.

MYRDAL, GUNNAR. *An American Dilemma.* New York: Harper and Brothers, 1944.

NELSON, JACK. *Values and Society.* Rochelle Park, N.J.: Hayden, 1975.

NEWMANN, FRED M., with DONALD W. OLIVER. *Clarifying Public Controversy: An Approach to Teaching Social Studies.* Boston: Little, Brown & Co., 1970.

OLIVER, DONALD W., and JAMES P. SHAVER. *Teaching Public Issues in the High School.* Boston: Houghton Mifflin, 1966.

PERLSTEIN, MARCIA H. (ed.). *Flowers Can Even Bloom in Schools.* Sunnyvale, Calif.: Westinghouse Learning Press, 1974.

PETERS, RICHARD S. *Ethics and Education.* Glenview, Ill.: Scott, Foresman, 1967.

PETERS, RICHARD S. "A Reply to Kohlberg," *Phi Delta Kappan,* June 1975, p. 678.

PHILLIPS, JAMES A., JR. *Developing Value Constructs in Schooling: Inquiry into Process and Product.* Worthington, Ohio: Ohio Association for Supervision and Curriculum Development, 1972.

PIAGET, JEAN. *The Moral Judgment of the Child.* London: Kegan Paul, Trench, Trubner & Co., Ltd., 1932.

PORTER, NANCY, and NANCY TAYLOR. *How to Assess the Moral Reasoning of Students.* Toronto: Ontario Institute for Studies in Education, 1972.

PURPEL, DAVID, and KEVIN RYAN. "Moral Education: Where Sages Fear to Tread," *Phi Delta Kappan,* June 1975, pp. 659–663.

RATHS, LOUIS E., MERRILL HARMIN, and SIDNEY B. SIMON. *Values and Teaching.* Columbus, Ohio: Charles E. Merrill, 1966.

REST, JAMES. "Developmental Psychology as a Guide to Value Education: A Review of 'Kohlbergian' Programs," *Review of Educational Research,* Spring 1974, pp. 241–259.

RICH, JOHN MARTIN. *Education and Human Values.* Reading, Mass.: Addison-Wesley, 1968.

ROKEACH, MILTON. *Beliefs, Attitudes and Values.* San Francisco: Jossey-Bass, 1970.

ROKEACH, MILTON. *The Nature of Human Values.* New York: The Free Press, 1973.

ROWE, MARY BUDD. *Teaching Science as Continuous Inquiry.* New York: McGraw-Hill, 1973.

RUGGIERO, VINCENT RYAN. *The Moral Imperative.* Port Washington, N.Y.: Alfred Publishing, 1973.

SCHRANK, JEFFREY. *Teaching Human Beings: 101 Subversive Activities for the Classroom.* Boston: Beacon Press, 1972.

SCRIVEN, MICHAEL. *Primary Philosophy.* New York: McGraw-Hill, 1966.

SCRIVEN, MICHAEL. *Value Claims in the Social Sciences.* Boulder, Colo.: Social Science Education Consortium, 1966.

SCRIVEN, MICHAEL. "Cognitive Moral Education," *Phi Delta Kappan,* June 1975.

SHAFTEL, FANNIE R., and GEORGE SHAFTEL. *Role-Playing for Social Values: Decision-Making in the Social Studies.* Englewood Cliffs, N.J.: Prentice-Hall, 1967.

SHAVER, JAMES P., and H. BERLAK. *Democracy, Pluralism, and the Social Studies: Readings and Commentary.* Boston: Houghton Mifflin, 1968.

SHAVER, JAMES P., and A. G. LARKINS. *Decision-Making in a Democracy.* Boston: Houghton Mifflin, 1973.

SHAVER, JAMES P., and WILLIAM STRONG. *Facing Value Decisions: Rationale-Building for Teachers.* Belmont, Calif.: Wadsworth, 1976.

SIMON, SIDNEY B., LELAND W. HOWE, and HOWARD KIRSCHENBAUM. *Values Clarification: A Handbook of Practical Strategies for Teachers and Students.* New York: Hart, 1972.

SIMPSON, ELIZABETH LEONIE. *Democracy's Stepchildren.* San Francisco: Jossey-Bass, 1971.

SIMPSON, ELIZABETH LEONIE. "Moral Development Research: A Case Study of Scientific Cultural Bias," *Human Development,* 1974, Vol. 17, pp. 81–106.

STEWART, JOHN S. "Clarifying Values Clarification: A Critique," *Phi Delta Kappan,* June 1975, pp. 684–689.

SUPERKA, DOUGLAS, et al. *Values Education Sourcebook: Conceptual Approaches, Materials Analyses, and an Annotated Bibliography.* Boulder, Colo.: ERIC Clearinghouse for Social Studies/Social Science Education and Social Science Education Consortium, 1976.

SUTHERLAND, EDWARD H. *White Collar Crime.* New York: Holt, Rinehart and Winston, 1949.

TURNBULL, COLIN. *The Mountain People.* New York: Simon & Schuster, 1972.

UBBELOHDE, CARL, and JACK R. FRAENKEL (eds.). *Values of the American Heritage: Challenges, Case Studies and Teaching Strategies.* Washington, D.C.: National Council for the Social Studies (46th Yearbook), 1976.

WADSWORTH, BARRY J. *Piaget's Theory of Cognitive Development: An Introduction for Students of Psychology and Education.* New York: David McKay, 1971.

WEHLAGE, GARY, and EUGENE M. ANDERSON. *Social Studies Curriculum in Perspective: A Conceptual Analysis.* Englewood Cliffs, N.J.: Prentice-Hall, 1972.

WEINSTEIN, GERALD, and MARIO D. FANTINI (eds.). *Toward Humanistic Education: A Curriculum of Affect.* New York: Praeger, 1970.

"Who Needs Rules?" Encyclopaedic Britannica Educational Corporation, Chicago, 1972.

WILSON, JOHN. *Language and the Pursuit of Truth.* Cambridge, Mass.: Cambridge University Press, 1967.